Manager's Guide to Motivating Employees

Other titles in the Briefcase Books series include:

To learn more about titles in the Briefcase Books series go to
www.briefcasebooks.com

Manager's Guide to Motivating Employees
Second Edition

Anne Bruce

McGraw-Hill

New York Chicago San Francisco Lisbon
London Madrid Mexico City Milan New Delhi
San Juan Seoul Singapore Sydney Toronto

ISBN   978-0-07-177297-6
MHID   0-07-177297-9

e-ISBN   978-0-07-177568-7
e-MHID   0-07-177568-4

This is a CWL Publishing Enterprises book developed for McGraw-Hill by CWL Publishing Enterprises, Inc., Madison, Wisconsin, www.cwlpub.com.

Product or brand names used this book may be trade names or trademarks. Where we believe there may be proprietary claims to such trade names or trademarks, the name has been used with an initial capital or it has been capitalized in the style used by the name claimant. Regardless of the capitalization used, all such names have been used in an editorial manner without any intent to convey endorsement of or other affiliation with the name claimant. Neither the author nor the publisher intends to express any judgment as to the validity or legal status of any such proprietary claims.

McGraw-Hill books are available at special quantity discounts to use as premiums and sales promotions, or for use in corporate training programs. To contact a representative, please e-mail us at bulksales@mcgraw-hill.com.

This book is printed on acid-free paper.

Contents

Acknowledgments

All 16 of the books I have authored would not have been possible if the audiences I speak to and train for did not quickly go to their iPhones, Blackberrys, iPads, or laptops, and start placing book orders with Amazon.com and other booksellers—sometimes before I even leave the stage.

Thank you to every person out there who has at one time or another attended one of my seminars, training events, workshops, or keynote speeches. And to all of you who keep coming back, bringing friends, and buying my books—without your support, there would not be another *Motivating Employees* Briefcase Book. Just know that the heartfelt stories you share with me, personal e-mails, letters, cards, and helpful feedback continue to enrich my life by allowing me to remain a part of yours.

Next, I have two families—the one I am related to by blood and friendship and the one I am related to via the publishing world. McGraw-Hill has been my publishing family for 16 years. To the amazing John Woods—you were my first editor and it's been an ongoing pleasure working with you and your team at CWL Publishing all these many years. I cut my teeth in this business learning from you and absorbing your guidance, wisdom, and philosophies as I've travelled the long and winding road of my publishing journey. Sure you're a super editor, but you're an even better dad, grandpa, husband, friend, and colleague.

If there were a book called *Motivated Friends and Family*, I'd be the author. You cannot write books for a living and fly more than 100,000 miles a year speaking on those books if you don't have the unconditional support and love from friends and family. I cannot list everyone, but you know who you are. Thank you from the bottom of my heart.

During the writing of this book, I had some very dedicated people come to my aid and stand by me when I was spinning many plates and trying not to drop any of them. You're the ones who got me through the deadlines of this year's projects, and I'd like to acknowledge you here. Thank you, thank you, thank you Jocelyn Godfrey! I'm so appreciative to have you in my cheering section. You're a brilliant writer, marketer, communications specialist, and loyal and dedicated friend. Your insights, cutting-edge ideas, super-fantastic attitude, and enormous contributions to this book while I was on the road and sending you chapters from 30,000 feet never ceased to amaze me. The revision of this book would not have been possible without you by my virtual side! You rock, lady! Also a special hug goes to Betty Garrett, president of Garrett Speakers International, for always believing in any new project I'm ready to launch and standing by my side through it all. Your ongoing advice, guidance, and generous heart—larger than the great state of Texas—have given my life deeper and truer meaning.

To my dearest friend Kim Lehner, during the writing of this book you jumped in and supported all of my other projects and events. You never let me feel alone for a second. I have loved you like a sister for 40 years— thank you from the bottom of my heart—and Jane Curtain thanks you, too! And to Diana Damron Monroe, your elegance and sophistication as a businesswoman, mom, wife, daughter, and friend have taught me so much through the years. You handle every life situation with decorum and grace. Remember, I was your biggest fan when you were a CBS anchorwoman, and I am even a bigger fan today!

And to my husband David, who encourages me to be more than I could ever dream possible. Thanks for being the hearth-hugger when I am the road warrior. I love playing house with you everyday. And finally, to the light that inspires me to shine in all that I do—my daughter, Autumn. Thank you for always believing in me. I am so proud of the beautiful and brilliant woman you are, both inside and out. I love you both more than I can express here.

This book is dedicated to my sister, Rose Marie Trammell, a woman who believes "Love never fails," and exemplifies it every day in her devotion to our family.

Introduction

Motivating your employees doesn't have to require heavy lifting, complex math, or aerospace engineering to get the stars to align. In fact, in this, the updated edition of this popular Briefcase Book, my aim is to make motivation more simple and fun than ever—while also keeping it incredibly practical. I've added insightful new material from today's top motivators and leaders—along with keeping some of the ageless wisdom from the best teachers and world-class motivators who've been around a while. I've kept the sections clear and concise—you can read them during your coffee breaks.

It's been more than a decade since the first-edition publishing of *Motivating Employees*, and today more than ever, a book like this one is needed to help managers navigate their way through turbulent times and periods of demanding change. Change has painted our world in many new layers and has impacted greatly how we motivate employees and teams. Since writing the first edition of *Motivating Employees*, world leaders left office amid nail-biting campaigns. Wars raged as leaders attempted to negotiate groundbreaking agreements. Tsunamis and earthquakes ravaged continents as countries valiantly rallied their citizens to create something new from the ruins. Corporate CEOs and politicians have fallen in corrupt scandals while society has questioned and improved leadership standards.

At the end of the day, all of us have had to dig deep to unveil our own unique, intrinsic motivation. In this new edition of my book, I've included a motivational diagnostic in Chapter 1 to help you continue the process and assist your employees in finding what motivates them to reach their highest level of performance and productivity. I believe it's the key to better performance, because when you know what motivates someone (and it's different for every person), you can fuel that intrinsic desire and kick things up a notch!

Breakneck Speed of Technology and Its Impact on Motivation

On the technology side of this past decade, we now carry stunningly sophisticated phones that keep track of our calendar, e-mail, social media, music library, photographs, and even grocery lists. Facebook, Twitter, LinkedIn, Google, and YouTube are all a click away and allow us to track long-lost friends, overseas relatives, or even coworkers—sometimes by the minute, or even the second. These flashy, tantalizing new gadgets and systems may make us more organized and connected than ever—but also may pull us into a land of distraction.

But through it all, while businesses merge, morph, evolve, or close doors, and technology upgrades shift our reality, fostering internal motivation has become a mainstay of management. During change or loss when no one is certain what wild catalyst might be just around the corner—or in the heart of technology overload—keeping your longstanding employees and new, young hires engaged and infused with traits like loyalty, dedication, and trust in leadership is challenging, yes, but also crucial and rewarding.

Imagine if you were to embark on a cross-sea adventure with a crew that was only slightly committed to your plan. Perhaps they were more committed to enjoying the ride or possibly finding a better ship along the way. What do you think would happen? Some of your key stakeholders might hang out down below playing poker and whooping it up while you plot your course. Then, when a big storm blows in with golf ball size–hail and high seas, you suddenly need all hands on deck. Would your employees arrive on the spot donning their foul weather gear to hoist (or take down) the sails and muscle up to get your boat to safe water? Or would they say, "The heck with this; we're goners anyway," and sing farewell songs as the seas rage—all the while cursing you for your lack of planning and training?

Now more than ever, Gallup and other organizations are publishing reports suggesting that employees are disengaged. Fear of change lurks like a wolf behind any number of trees in the forest up ahead, and many employees feel too paralyzed to take another step. Staying put—or worse, going below decks and waiting it out—can seem like a safer option.

These same studies, however, show that the success of an organization depends on keeping those employees motivated and involved. To make the journey in your project, goal, or effort, your employees must feel infused with motivation to stick with you through the storm—or whatever big or small challenges or detours you face.

Employee motivation starts by building trust and imparting the skills necessary so your employees can think on their feet and respond positively to challenges. Your employees are like your arms, legs, and eyes. You need them to function and move together in a way that is not whacky, but useful.

A Call to Action—It's Time to Turbocharge the Environment!

In the *Manager's Guide to Motivating Employees*, Second Edition, I'd like you to take this call to action by asking yourself the following: When was the last time you thought about really trying to "turn on" the people in your organization? You know, setting your employees on fire—inspiring them to be their best, to take risks, to think like entrepreneurs, and to unleash their limitless and synergistic potential. After all, you're the manager, right? Isn't that your job?

Well, yes, but it's different now in the twenty-first century. It's no longer up to you alone to provide for every employee's motivation. You now need to share this challenge with workers and let them share the responsibility for motivation. That's the focus of this book.

A manager's goal must be to help create a truly "motivating organization," one that inspires each employee to do his or her best every day—particularly when the manager isn't looking.

But you're probably thinking, "Hey, let's be practical. Who's got the time, and what's the magic formula?" Don't worry, I hear you loud and clear. I've been there, too.

Traveling more than 130,000 miles a year, speaking and conducting training on this subject, I do know what you're facing and what an incredible challenge it can be. I also realize that the thought of creating a motivating organization comes second when you get bogged down in day-to-day operations.

It's a dilemma for sure. I've observed how employees can become complacent as their jobs become more routine, more predictable over time. But I also know that the role you play as a leader and manager is extremely important! Your role creates your organization's motivating environment. In this book, I'm going to help you to turbocharge your environment to an even higher level of performance and productivity! Are you with me?

I wrote this book because I truly believe in the power and the influence that you can have. You're the manager! With the right tools and upgraded techniques, like the ones in this book, you can reawaken and revive the spirit in your organization. You can inspire all the people around you! You can create an environment in which employees will tap their own motivational energy to do their best work.

I wanted to write a revision of *Motivating Employees* to help you build a motivating organization—and to give you the tools to do it in real time! This book is not just meant to be read—it's meant to be used! This new edition Briefcase Book is not just a how-to-do-it field guide for motivating the workforce, it's also a what-to-do field guide for everyday use and practical application on the job.

It's no longer sufficient to give people simplistic, behavioral motivators. It just doesn't work to bring in a motivational speaker from time to time—no matter how great that consultant may be.

Employees today are better informed than ever before. They're too sophisticated for the quasimanipulative tactics that have worked for many managers in the past. Workers want greater satisfaction from their work. They're rarely "bought" with money alone or artificial rewards.

To successfully meet this new challenge, you, as a manager, must first understand the following issues, which I highlight throughout the book:

- Motivation is intrinsic—it emanates from within us.
- What we know about "human nature" explains why employees behave as they do.

- Managers should encourage an "entrepreneurial mind-set" and a feeling of "ownership" in all employees.
- Motivation leads to greater work performance.
- Every employee needs a clear understanding of his or her own particular motivation—a vision of hope and what life could be.
- Employees must attend to their own motivational needs.
- Employees want to do their jobs better when they love what they're doing.
- To sustain motivation, you need to attack the "de-motivators."
- Managers should have a better understanding of business systems and their impact on the people in the organization.
- The real power of teamwork is in the people—in their interests, motivations, and dynamics.
- Managers need to understand the power of synergy and how to unleash it.
- Motivating managers see their role as facilitator, trainer, and coach and they understand the important responsibility of preparing employees for change.

This Time We're Going to Turbocharge the Environment!

I believe that this book can help you become a more motivating manager. That means getting more done through people. After you've read this book, you'll be better equipped to build a highly motivated, higher-performing organization. You'll know how to facilitate powerful motivation within each of your employees. Plus, you'll understand how to focus on motivation at all levels—organization, teams, and individuals.

I hope you'll find this new and improved edition of *Motivating Employees* an invaluable resource that you'll refer to again and again in your work as a manager. It's my hope that, after reading the book, you'll be better able to create an environment in which your employees know what's expected of them and feel passionate about doing their jobs— motivated about putting the best of themselves into everything they do, and touching their greater potential one step at a time.

That's what I call a turbocharged workplace!

Special Features

The idea behind the books in the Briefcase Series is to give you practical information written in a friendly person-to-person style. The chapters deal with tactical issues and include lots of examples. They also feature numerous sidebars designed to give you different types of specific information. Here's a description of the sidebars you'll find in this book.

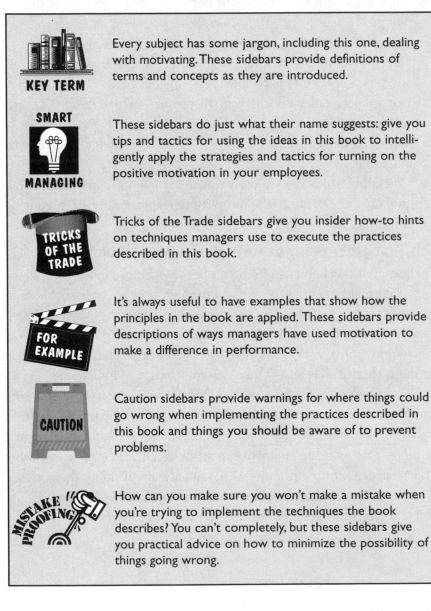

KEY TERM

Every subject has some jargon, including this one, dealing with motivating. These sidebars provide definitions of terms and concepts as they are introduced.

SMART MANAGING

These sidebars do just what their name suggests: give you tips and tactics for using the ideas in this book to intelligently apply the strategies and tactics for turning on the positive motivation in your employees.

TRICKS OF THE TRADE

Tricks of the Trade sidebars give you insider how-to hints on techniques managers use to execute the practices described in this book.

FOR EXAMPLE

It's always useful to have examples that show how the principles in the book are applied. These sidebars provide descriptions of ways managers have used motivation to make a difference in performance.

CAUTION

Caution sidebars provide warnings for where things could go wrong when implementing the practices described in this book and things you should be aware of to prevent problems.

MISTAKE PROOFING

How can you make sure you won't make a mistake when you're trying to implement the techniques the book describes? You can't completely, but these sidebars give you practical advice on how to minimize the possibility of things going wrong.

TOOLS

This icon identifies sidebars where you'll find specific procedures and techniques you can use to successfully implement the book's principles and practices.

Motivation Is an Inside Job

Top Talent and Their Characteristics Grow from the Inside Out

What is motivation? We typically define it as consisting of the drives that move us to do what we do. We have lots of drives. For example, if we're sitting around watching TV, our drives at that moment are for relaxation and entertainment. Our drives emanate from biological necessities, such as hunger and the desire to reproduce, and psychological needs, such as the need to feel acknowledged and valued by others and to accomplish worthwhile things in our lives.

People are motivated to do what they believe is in their best interests. This can often result in stupid, silly, or even unconsciously self-destructive behaviors. It can also result in brilliant achievements and great humanitarian acts. For most of us, most of the time, it results in the ordinary activities we engage in every day, usually with satisfactory results.

In thinking about motivation from a management perspective, it's important to appreciate this point: *You can't motivate other people. You can only influence what they're motivated to do.* That may seem like a sweeping statement, but this entire book is really about how to use that influence in a manner that results in employees feeling motivated to perform at high levels. Your goal as a manager should be to help employees identify their welfare with that of the organization. When that happens, they will naturally feel motivated to work hard—because it's in their best interests to do so.

As a manager interacting with employees, you should also appreciate that *it's impossible not to influence that motivation*, with either good or bad results for the organization. For example, if you are secretive and refuse to provide employees with the tools they believe they need, it's natural for employees to interpret this as a sign that you don't care about them, which leads them to care less about the company, which hurts their performance.

SMART MANAGING

AS MANAGER, YOU'RE A KEY INFLUENCER

It's important to remember that, one way or the other, you're going to affect your employees' motivation to perform. Often managers are oblivious to this fact. But if you understand and acknowledge this reality then you can act in ways that positively affect their motivation to perform at higher levels and work more effectively with others.

To be a key influencer means that by virtue of your reputation, your status, your position in the organization, your reputation, or your relationships, you are a key person who can help shift people's paradigms and behaviors. Throughout your management career you will want to identify other key influencers when they come along. Those are the people who can help you achieve your goals, move projects forward, and create motivational buzz around new ideas and announcements.

The question you need to ask, then, as a manager is, "As a key influencer am I positively or negatively influencing my employees' motivation?" The ideas you'll read here are all about helping you learn how to positively influence what your employees are motivated to do.

Motivation: Intrinsic and Extrinsic

Motivation, as most people approach the concept, is *intrinsic*—it's inside us. We feel a desire or drive to do something, and we behave in ways to accomplish that.

But we don't operate in a vacuum. We live in the world and what we experience affects us. In other words, our motivation is affected by external factors. Those factors can include rewards, recognition, bonuses, promotions, and praise. On the job, it's great to take joy in what we're doing, but if there aren't any pay incentives or appreciation for our efforts, we're likely to wonder if such activities are worth the time we spend on them.

We call these external aspects of motivation *extrinsic*. They affect our *intrinsic* motivation to do something. But make no mistake about it: whatever we do, it's always because we believe it will fulfill some current or future personal goal or desire we have.

KEY TERMS

Intrinsic Factors that motivate us from within—such as personal interest, desire, and fulfillment.

Extrinsic Factors outside us that influence our internal needs, wants, and subsequent behaviors—such as rewards, promotions, and praise.

We often refer to extrinsic factors as motivating forces, but that's not quite accurate. Whatever part these external factors play in motivation, they're always subject to our individual, intrinsic concerns—that is, we have to buy into them.

That buy-in means that we must make a connection between our intrinsic motivation and extrinsic stimuli. Without this connection, receiving rewards won't motivate high performance over the long term. Instead, people will work only until they receive the reward—and once they do, they'll stop. For example, a production manager offers a bonus if her employees can deliver a certain quantity of outputs by a certain date. They may succeed, but once they get the bonus, they have no reason to continue working at this level.

DOES YOUR MOTIVATION COME FROM WITHIN?

FOR EXAMPLE

Do you believe that motivation always comes from within? Think about your own experience. When have you been most excited about your work? When have you worked your hardest and enjoyed it the most? For most of us, it was when we were involved in projects we took personally—projects in which we felt we could really accomplish something for ourselves and those we worked with. We identified personally with the project and felt that by doing a good job on it, we were doing something for ourselves. That's intrinsic motivation at work.

Happiness as a Motivator

In *The Happiness Advantage*, author Shawn Achor, who spent more than a decade researching and teaching this subject at Harvard, illustrates how the field of positive psychology has shown that happiness doesn't magically arrive when we have the right car, house, spouse, or job.

Instead, he states, "Happiness fuels success, not the other way around. When we are positive, our brains become more engaged, creative, motivated, energetic, resilient, and productive at work. This isn't just an empty mantra. This discovery has been repeatedly borne out of rigorous research in psychology and neuroscience, management studies, and the bottom lines of organizations around the globe."

So when we talk about motivating employees, we're really trying to help them make that connection between their inner drives to fulfill their personal needs and what that might mean in terms of working hard and smart on the job. In effect, we are trying to activate their inner happiness, so that they can attract and achieve success. When employees identify their own joy and welfare with those of their employer, as noted above, they'll naturally work harder.

The 3As of Intrinsic Motivation

Intrinsic motivation doesn't have to be complicated, but it helps to have a basic road map. Doug McKinley, Psy.D., corporate trainer and coauthor (with Sam Glenn and Scott Carbonara) of *Go Positive: Lead to Engage*, proposes a "3A" approach to turning on employee intrinsic motivation. Before implementing the 3As with a team, however, McKinley's group urges managers first to adopt the principles into their own work and lives. Leaders who clear the trail by implementing the principles themselves not only model positive behavior for their employees, but also ensure that they are engaged as managers. After all, motivating employees is a tricky feat if you as a leader suffer from disengagement.

Activating the 3As

1. Awareness. Engaged employees adopt awareness of the core values of the organization, and are alert to its mission and goals. What big questions is your company answering? How is your group contributing to the improvement of life on our planet? Find and define the deeper purpose, and spread it to your team members.

2. Alignment. Under this principle, employees align their own purpose and job description with the organization's values and goals, so that they are personally invested in their tasks and the outcome. To optimize engagement, an employee's personal goals should align with those of the business. For example, an employee who values sobriety would probably not be in alignment while working for a liquor company! People feel more motivated to work hard when they understand how their work adds value to the organization, when they can appreciate how what they're doing contributes to the work community, and when they believe in the work they are accomplishing. If you help your employees take interest and pride in their work, you'll find the investment to be worthwhile. It's even better if you can match the job to the employee. Here's a tip on implementing alignment: help your employees define not only how their roles fit into the bigger picture within your company, but also how their jobs tie into their own life legacies.

3. Action. Once awareness and alignment are established, encourage and reward action toward deliverables. All the motivation and theory in the world won't actually build or sell a new product, but mind and muscle power will!

People feel more motivated to work hard when they feel empowered to make decisions about their work. Find ways to allow and encourage your employees to make decisions, and provide them with the support and tools they need to do their work.

You may find it easy to get caught up in the hoopla of what gets employees revved up and excited. You might quickly become obsessed with finding the right incentive—a bonus, a raise, a new office, an extra day of vacation. But it's more critical to concentrate on the factors that will affect an employee's enthusiasm for the work—factors that are within each employee. These factors are more likely to promote positive action.

USE THE 3As   SMART

You can help your employees find greater motivation through the 3As—awareness, alignment, action. There are many MANAGING tactics that can assist in this process. Encourage employees to fulfill their value for affiliation, for example, by developing teamwork and spirit. Make their jobs more interesting and challenging, for example, by giving them different tasks to do on different days. Empower them to feel a sense of control and achievement, for example, by giving them authority to spend up to $500 without approval for materials, tools, and supplies.

Intrinsic Motivation and Creating a Bond with the Organization

An employee who feels a bond with the organization will volunteer to stay late at work to finish an important task, even though this may interfere with planned personal activities at home.

If you try to motivate employees primarily by offering extrinsic rewards, then it's unlikely they'll feel much like staying late. Instead, you'll make people feel like they're doing their jobs to please the organization, not themselves. You're probably familiar with this scenario: "Hey, that's not my job. Why should I stay late? What's in it for me?" Sound familiar?

Think about it. Why do employees sometimes seem like they're not motivated to perform very well for you? Do you recognize any of the following reasons in your workplace?

- Organizational fear or intimidation
- Bureaucracy or red tape
- Deadline pressures and anxiety
- Conflicting goals and messages within the organization
- Lack of training
- Disputes between unionized workers and management
- Conflicts between short-term and long-term organizational goals
- Lack of direction
- Unclear objectives
- Lack of time and resources to do the job
- Management not valuing frontline staff and their contributions

Would you feel motivated under such circumstances? Probably not. On the other hand, you might be thinking about "problem" employees you've experienced. You might be saying, "For some people, it's all just a way to make a living—another day, another dollar. It's not easy to manage people like that." You're right. It's not. But how much are *your* attitude and behavior influencing *their* attitudes and behaviors? If you look for problem people, you'll find them. But you can also look for the strengths in those same people.

For example, you can go to Dallas, Boston, or Tucson and find the most objectionable and negative people in the world. Or you can go to

Dallas, Boston, or Tucson and find the most motivated, enthusiastic, and positive people in the world. The point is that you can look for the good qualities and find them in abundance—even in people who are apparently bored, discouraged, or unwilling to do anything for anybody.

MOTIVATING THROUGH TEAMWORK

SMART MANAGING

People feel more motivated to work hard when they're inspired to cooperate and when they have an opportunity to help one another succeed. If you eliminate obstacles that hold individuals responsible for the success or failure of a project, you'll create an environment that encourages natural motivation and team spirit.

Kick Up Employee Motivation and Performance Using This Easy Assessment

This is a powerful and important assessment you can easily facilitate for your employees and teams. Remember that each of us is motivated by something different. Sally may be motivated by praise and recognition, and Sam might be motivated by the result of a job well done. The key is in asking your people what motivates them individually to their higher level of peak performance and productivity. What you're asking is, "What matters to you most?"

When an employee shares that information with you, you will hold the golden key to building morale and turbocharging the workplace. Here's how.

Think about it. If you know what fuels a person's desire to do better, you hold the secret to stoking the fires of passion and intrinsic motivation. If Sally says that praise and recognition motivate her, then you can accommodate that desire when Sally performs well by praising her progress and recognizing her efforts on the spot. If Sam tells you that he's stoked by the result of a job well done, then when he's completed a project and has excelled at it, you can affirm the results with him. That's powerful in-the-moment coaching. Knowing that Sam is motivated by a sense of accomplishment for having done his job well, you now have everything you need to motivate him even further and increase his likelihood to perform and produce at higher levels more consistently.

Using This Powerful Motivation Tool

Ask your employees to rank on a scale of 1 to 4 what motivates them to their highest level of performance and productivity, with 4 being the highest rating. Next, have them select only from the motivators that rated 4, their three most important motivators. Finally, have them select the single greatest motivator. Tell them to place a big star next to it. Explain that you are aware there is overlap in some of these descriptions. However, you still want them to laser focus on the single most important motivating factor that really turns them on to doing a super fantastic job!

Debrief for More Valuable Information

Now debrief with your team or employee. Ask him or her what it is about what they chose that makes them want to be their best and increase their level of productivity and performance. When managers ask their people questions like these, they will always get an answer. This information is not a secret! So ask! Use this information to help fuel your employees and motivate them to peak performance!

Think back to when you started out in your career. Can you imagine how you might have felt if your manager would have asked you these questions? Do you think you would have felt more valued as a worker? Would you have felt more cared about? Do you think you might have felt more enthusiastic about your work as a result? Would you have tried harder? If you answer yes, then you've just validated the importance of assessing employees' needs when it comes to what motivates them most.

A final note: Compensation is listed because it is indeed among the many things that motivate us. We all have to raise our families and pay our bills. However, it's rarely the #1 motivating factor that gets people to move out of bed early to do a great job, work long hours, or give the company their best. You may find an employee or two who selects compensation as their primary motivator, but it is rare. Most people are motivated by other things. If you have a team member who is only motivated by money, then find a second primary motivator for him or her to focus on. Acknowledge that they have the prerogative to select compensation as their #1 motivation, but if you aren't in a position to raise his or her salary, then a second motivating factor needs to be identified.

SELF-ASSESSMENT: MOTIVATION DIAGNOSTIC FOR EMPLOYEES

On a scale from 1 to 4, with 4 being the highest rating and 1 being the lowest rating, assign a number to what motivates you to your highest level of performance.

1. My leadership showing concern for me as a person	4	3	2	1
2. Good working relationship with my leadership	4	3	2	1
3. Empowerment and tools to get the job done	4	3	2	1
4. Leader's ability to make decisions	4	3	2	1
5. Leader who "Walks the Talk"	4	3	2	1
6. Recognition of my efforts	4	3	2	1
7. Delegation of responsibility to me	4	3	2	1
8. Being promoted	4	3	2	1
9. Contact with people	4	3	2	1
10. Compensation	4	3	2	1
11. Getting along with others	4	3	2	1
12. Honest praise and feedback	4	3	2	1
13. Constructive and corrective feedback	4	3	2	1
14. Coaching and career counseling	4	3	2	1
15. The result of a job well done	4	3	2	1
16. Attending social functions with team members	4	3	2	1
17. Being given clear objectives	4	3	2	1
18. Job security	4	3	2	1
19. Mobile technology	4	3	2	1
20. (Something not on this list: add here) _____	4	3	2	1

It's a fact of human nature: people are always motivated. The big question is, what are they motivated to do? The key for you is to create an environment where employees feel motivated to do a great job every day. Here are some tips for doing that and winning the cooperation of employees:

- Build self-esteem in others by complimenting them on good work.
- Show patience and concern.
- Ask for input, then do something with it.
- Let employees share responsibility for improving work processes and train them to do this.
- Appreciate the quiet workers, as well as the extroverts.
- Share your vision and ask for ideas from others.
- Teach others how to do things themselves and encourage them to do so.
- Tie raises to performance, not to seniority.

- Allow and encourage lateral moves.
- Encourage problem solving and support the solutions employees come up with.
- Show how employees' efforts are meaningful by showing them how their work adds value for the organization.
- Interact and communicate with people.
- Give employees something to be excited about.

Ask, "What's in It for Them?"

If you really want to influence people's motivation, you have to uncover their reasons for doing things, their purposes, and their causes. People aren't going to be truly motivated for *your* reasons and goals. Employees ask themselves, "What's in it for me?" It's your responsibility to find out what their motives are and to then help them connect those to organizational goals and activities. And that will positively affect their performance on the job.

CAUTION

NOT ALL EMPLOYEES GET IT

You can never expect all employees to identify with the company or spark their motivation to perform at the levels you'd like. Give those people tasks best suited to their abilities and drive. In an environment with enthusiastic, committed employees, those who don't feel this way will usually leave the organization because they don't fit in. When you have employees whose attitude and behavior seems to drag down everyone else, you'll need to have a serious talk with them about their future with the company.

If you do this well, employees will start asking, "What's in it for us?" Why? Because when you're looking out for their interests, they'll see that looking out for the organization is how they look out for themselves. It may take time for this to happen, but most employees will come around if you persist.

Create an Environment of Intrinsic Motivation Through Self-Discovery

Dolly Hinshaw is a highly regarded and successful businesswoman who's often referred to as having "the edge" when it comes to creating departmental collaboration for her clients. As founder of Hinshaw & Associates, a sales training and high-performance leadership consulting and strategic-planning organization, Dolly is no stranger to motivation in the workplace. In fact, she takes it a step further by encouraging clients to create work environments of self-discovery.

Based in the greater Chicago area, with more than 20 years of sales and operations experience, Dolly combines out-of-the-box thinking with an in-depth knowledge of the marketplace to help clients and their employees celebrate success with enthusiastic behavior and a high level of intrinsic motivation.

"Employee motivation grows from a person's own drive for success and happiness. It's intrinsic in every way. Leaders guiding employees to exceed company expectations need to inspire them to increase their own self-motivation in wanting to enhance their performance. Tapping into employees' intrinsic motivation while creating *environments of self-discovery* is the secret every leader should incorporate into building an innovative atmosphere. Influencing another person's journey to increase their own self-motivation is the greatest gift a leader can bestow on his or her workers," says Hinshaw.

Eight Steps to Creating Environments of Self-Discovery

1. **Live the Standards.** Make a personal commitment as manager to inspire productivity by setting the standards of excellence in being able to demonstrate successful skills to get results. Ensure that organizational values are shared and always mentor expected behavior.

2. **Focus on Behaviors.** Continuously improve your observational skills. Pay attention to body language, verbal communication skills, technical expertise, cultural sensitivities, training capacities, team building, others' responses, and more.

3. **Cultivate Skills.** Encourage training and education, demonstrate appropriate skill sets via role simulations, expand horizons by creating opportunities for growth, and inspire confidence with positive feedback. Demonstrate that you welcome feedback, as well.

4. **Share Creative Pathways.** Ignite the passion for using new methods, building more collaborative teams, creating more innovative techniques,

embracing technology, enhancing communication tools, and more. Provide physical environments conducive to idea generation.

5. Diffuse Stress. Get to know individual and team triggers that create stress. Get to know individual team members and treat everyone with fairness and respect. Personal attention is key to inspiring self-motivation.

6. Communicate by Design. Everyone welcomes communication from their leaders. How much and how often needs to be customized based on preferences and performance levels.

7. Challenge Beyond Comfort Zones. Once a person has mastered certain tasks, they risk getting bored or stagnant. Extending people beyond their comfort zone is as important to them as it is to the organization. Creating opportunities to learn new skills is paramount to future success.

8. Celebrate Success. All milestones on an employee's journey to promotion need acknowledgment. This provides the motivation to keep moving forward. Leaders need to embrace the previous seven steps to collaboratively celebrate in this success.

According to Hinshaw, inner, personal motivation is a continuous process. Keeping employees enthusiastic requires rewards of new responsibilities, promotions, and new challenges. By using these eight steps in creating "environments of self-discovery," leaders will be personally rewarded in knowing that they have inspired new leaders in developing more innovative products and services in the future.

Visit www.hinshaw-associates.com for performance models, white papers, productivity tools, motivational strategies, and more.

THE HINSHAW MODEL

Dolly Hinshaw has developed a model for building distinctive characteristics of high-performing workers and their teams. High-performance teams deliver cutting-edge results for the organizations whose leaders inspire their empowerment. These teams are composed of individuals who are highly self-motivated. There are common characteristics associated with these individuals. Enhancing the skills associated with these characteristics is the link to optimal results.

Distinctive Characteristics of High-Performance Employees

Supportive. Withholds judgments and listens to different perspectives. Supportive qualities include understanding and trust.

Energetic. Enjoys challenges, dispels negative thoughts, and enjoys life.

Leading-Edge Thinker Seeks diverse points of view for insight, is progressive, and explores what the future might look like. Takes risks.

Focused. Observant, deals with obstacles, interruptions, and setbacks with ease and certainty. Keeps cool under pressure.

Mature. Trusts and respects the alignment of vision-goals-process team. Self assesses and evaluates to increase performance.

Optimistic. Works hard to maximize success, learns from mistakes, and is proactive to make changes for a better outcome.

Team Player. Believes in the synergy of ideas, collaborative discussion, balance of participation, compromise, and consensus decision making.

Intelligent. Has excellent knowledge of organization's products and services, understands goals and processes, and expresses themselves clearly. Has the ability to think beyond the next step.

Value Oriented. Creates best practices and standards of excellence, lives by their priority virtues, and believes in the mission and vision of the organization. Virtues may include patience, fairness, humility, determination, and integrity.

Accountable. Is productive, communicates with precision, meets deadlines, and absorbs critiques. Some tools to assist with accepting responsibility are listening, asking clarifying questions, giving and receiving feedback, and being straightforward in a positive way.

Tenacious. Has the drive and commitment to excel and accomplish any goal set before them. Turns ideas into actions and never gives up.

Enthusiastic. Represents themselves with a positive self-image and has a true passion about their organization.

Dedicated. Is committed to their responsibilities by continuously improving on and expanding the characteristics on the "distinctive characteristics" list of high performance.

Self-motivation is driven by an excitement of much more than earning bonuses or promotions. It is driven by having a stake in the success and accomplishment of realizing personal achievement and being part of an organizational culture that challenges its employees to be more innovative than the competition.

No One Craves Mediocrity—Employees Require Confidence to Excel!

Organizations, big and small, are not craving mediocrity. The world is not hungry for people who do so-so jobs. Below average, doesn't cut it. Organizations need confident workers with healthy self-images. As a manager in your organization you have tremendous power when it comes to instill-ing or building self-esteem among your workers. By the same token, you hold the same power to crush your worker's self-confidence depending on how you speak to and treat them day in and day out.

Managers of successful corporations, nonprofit organizations, and government agencies know that instilling confidence in their people does not happen by focusing on their weaknesses and tearing down their self-esteem. Confident workers develop by maximizing and growing their unique talents and strengths. When managers focus on people's natural talents and strengths, they build self-confidence in their people. They help employees develop stronger self-esteem and a healthy self-image.

BEWARE OF LOW MOTIVATION

CAUTION Self-motivation combined with confidence lifts employees and organizations to new heights, and the lack of these traits holds employees back.

Be aware of employees who lack self-motivation and self-confidence, and who demonstrate low self-esteem or minimal self-worth. The combination of these traits can be disastrous and lead to complacency and oftentimes a bad attitude that affects productivity and performance on the job. Just like an airplane sitting out on the runway with empty fuel tanks, it may be a perfectly good airplane, but without fuel, it's not going to get off the ground, let alone soar and reach its ultimate destination. Self-motivation and self-confidence are fuel to an employee. As manager, it's your job to fill the tanks of your employees and help each person to soar!

The Three Most Common Ways to Influence Motivation

Managers usually try to influence employee motivation, with both posi-tive and negative results, in one of three ways: by using fear, incentives, and, occasionally, the opportunity for personal growth. Let's explore each of these approaches briefly and the results they're likely to generate.

Fear Motivation

Fear motivation usually peaks when the economy is sluggish and there are more qualified workers than jobs available. For example, in a com-pany where jobs are in jeopardy, many workers will consciously make a greater effort to be productive, arrive earlier, stay later, or do more than the job requires.

When workers are motivated by fear, they're not so much trying to achieve something as they're trying to avoid losing their jobs. This approach to motivation might work temporarily, and it can spark an increase in organizational productivity.

The potential trap in taking this approach is that the results typically won't last. In fact, over the long run, using fear to influence employees' motivation can even backfire on the organization. If you use fear in an attempt to get employees to perform, you'll find that they will get used to it to the point where fear becomes the primary emotion they connect to life on the job. This can lead to intense dislike and resentment, which undermine cooperation and communication. And in the worst cases, it can even cause sabotage.

Incentive Motivation

Another common approach to motivating employees is dangling a carrot. Managers hold some kind of incentive in front of employees in hopes of getting them to move forward to get the reward. It's such a standard technique that you might not think much about how difficult it is to make incentives work over the long haul. People will work to get the reward. But what happens after they've received it?

The potential trap in this approach is that employees will continue to want a reward to do any of their tasks. You have to keep coming up with new and better rewards to get them to do their work. They can come to expect more and more rewards and, if you don't provide those rewards, they won't do much beyond the minimum.

Personal Growth Motivation

When you look at personal growth as a motivator, you change the way your employees think about their work, you help them become more capable, and you give them a meaningful purpose in coming to work. The opportunity for personal growth is one of the keys to maximizing employee motivation. It's one way to plug into the natural human tendency to look out for ourselves. Later in this book, you'll learn some ways to help your employees personally grow on the job.

Relationships: A Key to Better Performance

We cannot and must not manage people as we might manage a budget or an account. The very nature of the relationships you build will directly influence what your employees are motivated to do in the workplace. So let's reiterate the point I made early in this chapter: *you don't motivate people; you influence what they're motivated to do.*

Manager's Checklist for Chapter 1

☑ People are motivated to do what they believe is in their best interests.

☑ You can't motivate another person. You can only influence what he or she is motivated to do. And, as a manager, you're going to influence that motivation, either positively or negatively. So pay attention and take actions that will have a positive effect.

☑ People talk about motivation as being intrinsic or extrinsic, but it's really only intrinsic within each of us. What we call extrinsic motivation is really just external factors that affect our intrinsic motivation.

☑ Doug McKinley stresses the 3As of employee engagement—awareness, alignment, action. People feel more motivated to work hard when they're aware of the organization's goals and values, when they understand how their work contributes to the organization, and when they feel empowered to make decisions about their work.

☑ The three forms of motivation that managers use most often are fear, incentives, and the opportunity for personal growth. The first two can undermine motivation to perform. The last can help you encourage your employees to feel motivated to perform at high levels.

Working with Human Nature

Know What Employees Need to Thrive

We all depend on our personal motivation to sustain our efforts in any activity. Without personal motivation, situations generally look worse and actions seem more difficult.

Psychologist and philosopher William James said, "The deepest principle in human nature is the craving to be appreciated." James suggested that an effective leader brings people closer to alliance by demonstrating a concern for their personal values and motivations. Today this approach is considered vital when dealing with employees.

As a leader in your organization, you must gain a better understanding of human nature and why people behave as they do. By investing time in this effort, you'll become better equipped to relate to your employees—and you'll build a more productive and enjoyable work environment. It's called nurturing nature.

Why, What, When, and How Things Happen

Sometimes we just can't understand some people! What they do may surprise us. What they don't do may disappoint us. What they do in unexpected ways may frustrate us. But if you explore some basic theories of human nature, it will be easier for you to find the answers to why, what, when, and how things happen in your particular work environment.

Theories? How can theories help you make sense out of what people do? Well, that depends on how you use them. It's true that theories of human nature can never predict with certainty what people will do or how they will act. But theories can indicate what might happen and give you useful guidelines for handling various situations—thus reducing the surprise, the disappointment, or the frustration.

The Concept of Theory X and Theory Y

In *The Human Side of Enterprise* (1960), Douglas McGregor described a new way to explain how managers might view workers according to different concepts of human nature as applied to work. He described two alternatives, *Theory X* and *Theory Y*. These concepts can best be imagined as opposite extremes on a continuum.

In his highly acclaimed book, McGregor asserted that managers who buy into Theory X make the following assumptions:

- Work is inherently distasteful.
- The average person is lazy and unambitious.
- People prefer close supervision.
- Typical workers avoid responsibility.
- The principal worker incentive is money.
- Workers must be coerced or bribed to achieve the organization's goals.

In sharp contrast, McGregor argued that managers who subscribe to Theory Y make the following assumptions:

- People enjoy work.
- Work is as natural as play.
- Recognition and self-fulfillment are as important as money.
- Employees are committed to their work.
- Employees exercise self-direction and seek responsibility.
- Workers at all levels will exhibit creativity and ingenuity when given the chance.

OK, now take a moment to think about how *you* act toward your employees, how *you* treat them, how *you* talk about them. Just imagine a typical day or week, then watch what you do and listen to what you say. Where would you be on the Theory X–Theory Y continuum? At the end with Theory X? At the end with Theory Y? Somewhere in between, maybe? If so, are you closer to one end or the other?

Theory X and Theory Y describe the different assumptions managers make about what people are like. And it's not just theoretical, of course, because we act on these assumptions; we treat our employees according to our beliefs about human nature.

Your assumptions as a manager will have a signifi-

KEY TERM

McGregor's Theory X Assumes that work is inherently distasteful, people are lazy and unambitious, workers prefer close supervision and avoid responsibility, money is the principle incentive, and workers must be coerced or bribed.

McGregor's Theory Y Assumes that people enjoy work, work is as natural as play, recognition and self-fulfillment are as important as money, employees are committed to their work and exercise self-direction and seek responsibility, and workers will show creativity and ingenuity when given the chance.

cant impact on the relationships you develop with your employees and on the ways you'll try to improve their motivation. These managerial attitudes affect how you interact with the people working around you, how you manage people, and how you influence the work environment—intentionally or subconsciously.

Understanding Your Personal Style of Management

The sets of assumptions that McGregor labeled as Theory X and Theory Y are extremes on a continuum. There are probably no managers who are a pure X or Y. But this approach to management beliefs should help you better understand your natural management style—your management instincts, if you will. It might also help you appreciate when your attitudes might adjust to a specific situation, within a particular environment, in a given culture, or with certain employees.

So it's not really a question of whether you're a Theory X manager or a Theory Y manager. Each type has to get the job done working with and through people. The key to success is determining which style of managing is most consistent with bringing out the highest levels of motivation in your employees.

The Theory X management style represents trusting only yourself to do the right things. In terms of how you relate to employees, we can say it's a *control-oriented* approach to managing. The Theory Y management style demonstrates a trust in both yourself and your employees to do the right thing by each other. In terms of how you relate to employees, we can say it's an *empowerment-oriented* approach to managing.

Let's review the differences between these two management styles.

Control-Oriented, In-It-for-Them Manager (Theory X Approach):

- In it for them first.
- Makes decisions without the input of others.
- Maintains control.
- Is confident in the validity of his or her views.
- Is goal-oriented and sometimes demanding.
- May use pressure to reach objectives.
- May use discipline with those who don't do the job correctly.
- Acts decisively and can confront poor performance.
- Expects no criticism from the team.

Empowerment-Oriented, Gives-Power-Away Manager (Theory Y Approach):

- Gives power away.
- Makes decisions by consensus and helps others feel "ownership."
- Encourages creativity and initiative.
- Coaches others and effectively facilitates the work of others.
- Leads by example.
- Gives recognition for work done well.
- Helps people grow in their work and gain more responsibility.
- Values and encourages teamwork.

If your management style leans toward Theory X, you more than likely interact with your employees in a way that affirms this theory and creates a Theory X environment. You probably press people to perform, instruct them every step of the way, and tell them what to do and how to do it. You look over their shoulder and they resent it, reacting negatively to your constant direction and control. Of course, this resentment reinforces your belief that employees do have to be micromanaged if you want the job done right.

In other words, Theory X assumptions become fact. You might not even realize that you're creating a Theory X environment that employees are adapting to—which is why understanding these theories is critical to becoming an effective manager. It doesn't make much sense to create an environment that will give you lower levels of performance than you want.

The opposite is true if your management style leans toward Theory Y. Because of what you assume about employees, you'll build a climate of mutual trust, giving them the authority and responsibility to do their jobs as well as they can. And you can also expect employees to react positively to being treated with respect and receiving the support they need to perform well. Again, we see a case of assumptions becoming fact here.

Theory Y is about an attitude you take toward interacting with your employees. Think for a moment about all the people around you—particularly the employees you supervise but also your fellow managers and your bosses. People will have varying degrees of experience, energy levels, and interests in the jobs they're performing. So it's not logical to assume that a Theory Y manager can give everyone, without exception, the responsibility to perform as they see fit or to make important decisions that affect the whole department or organization.

You'll often have to adjust your behavior to the needs of your individual employees as well as the specific circum-

WHEN THEORY X MAY BE REQUIRED
You may need to take a highly directive approach (more like Theory X) when employees are misusing or abusing their authority to the detriment of others, when employees are neglecting organizational policies and jeopardizing work groups, or when there's an emergency situation that endangers safety.

SMART MANAGING

ATTITUDE IS ALL

In some situations as a manager, you'll have to be very directive, even if you understand the importance of the Theory Y approach. That's OK. The important thing is your attitude. Your attitude as a manager will drive your employees' choices and ultimately their behaviors.

Theory Y managers direct people to help them succeed, not simply to be the boss. Your attitude in dealing with people is crucial. If you have an attitude of helping employees succeed and giving them what they need to do that, most employees will sense that and be receptive.

stances you're dealing with. You've got to use your best judgment and common sense as appropriate to the time, the place, the circumstances, and the individuals involved.

Look at it this way. If your building were to catch on fire, you wouldn't stop to reach a consensus on who should call the fire department, who should use the extinguisher, and so forth. On the other hand, if you're facilitating a brainstorming session, don't expect great results if you simply demand creative solutions and pressure participants to provide them immediately.

Human Needs and Response

As a manager, you'll benefit from understanding the McGregor concept of Theory X and Theory Y in terms of how you can interact effectively with employees and what you can expect from such interactions. But what is it that drives the behavior of any person? A widely accepted answer to that question comes from Abraham Maslow, a well-known and respected behavioral scientist.

As emphasized earlier, we're all motivated from within. But what are the internal forces that motivate us? Maslow attempted to answer this question by studying the *needs* that motivate human behavior. He arranged these needs into several levels, his *Hierarchy of Needs*, according to their importance to our survival.

He suggested that the internal factors that first motivate us are our basic *physiological needs*—our needs for food, shelter, water, and air. The next level in his hierarchy is the need for *security* or *safety*, so that we might feel protected from danger or harm. The third level is *social*, including our

need to be loved, to belong to a
group, and to have the respect
of others. The fourth level is
the *ego*, where self-esteem,
status, prestige, and recognition come into play. Finally, we
have *self-actualization*, the
need to realize our personal
potential and become all that
we can with whatever we've
got.

Maslow's Hierarchy of Needs The structure Abraham Maslow devised for understanding different **KEY TERM** types of human needs. Human beings must first fulfill those needs at the lower end of the hierarchy before being concerned with those at the higher end. From bottom to top, the levels are physiological needs, needs for security or safety, social needs, ego needs, and the need for self-actualization.

Linking Performance with Individual Needs

So what can you, as a manager, gain from Maslow? You can learn how to improve a worker's performance by linking job behaviors with the satisfaction of that worker's individual needs. People are motivated to do a job well when it helps them meet one or more of their personal needs.

The challenge for you is that different people have different needs, and those needs change over time and according to the context of the situation. But you can certainly use your understanding of the Hierarchy of Needs as a guide. Now, let's consider the impact of Maslow's theory in creating a workplace where people feel fulfilled and want to work productively.

Gallup's Q12 Research

Between Theory X and Theory Y, does one management style help create a more positive, engaging work environment—one where employees reach their full potential and become self-actualized? According to the Gallup Organization's Q12 research, the answer is *yes*. Its groundbreaking research involving hundreds of focus groups and thousands of interviews showed a strong correlation between high employee engagement levels and high employee performance levels.

From its research, Gallup refined 12 questions. High-performing employees answered these questions with the strongest possible positive affirmation. What kind of questions linked engagement to performance? Were these questions about satisfaction with pay, benefits, or other perks?

No. Check out some of these:

- Do you know what is expected of you at work?
- In the last seven days, have you received recognition or praise for doing good work?
- Does your supervisor, or someone at work, seem to care about you as a person?
- Is there someone at work who encourages your development?
- At work, do your opinions seem to count?

Doesn't this sound more like a Theory Y leader? It does.

Again, emergency situations call for more highly directive leadership styles. In combat, for example, there's no time to reach consensus, nor would it be desirable to have each soldier express his or her feelings about the battle objectives! But when it comes to day-in, day-out leadership, employees are more apt to engage and gravitate toward leaders who ask them to come along instead of demanding it.

Know What Drives People

As a manager, you should know what drives your employees. If you put people in jobs where they can meet their individual needs while doing the work that's important to the organization, you'll have employees who are more motivated to perform well. Regardless of the type of work employees do, you can take steps to help them feel a sense of control over that work and its importance to the organization. Now is a good time to go back and review the Self-Assessment: Motivation Diagnostic in Chapter 1. How can you use your employees' responses in this assessment to help you to better understand what really drives them further, faster, and to a higher level of performance and productivity?

How can you identify the needs of your employees? And how do you know if and how those needs are being met? Consider the following recommendations:

- Watch people doing their jobs. What turns them on or off? How do they prefer doing things? Give them the opportunity to use their own methods as long as they're compatible with effectively getting the job done.
- Set up employee focus groups to find out what they would like from their work. Have them brainstorm ways to make work more fulfilling.

HIGHER NEEDS = HIGHER MOTIVATION   SMART

The higher the need satisfied by any work activity, the greater the motivation to perform that activity—and the more the activity will mean to the employee. The smart manager thinks in terms of helping the job first meet his or her employees' lower-level   MANAGING
needs, then thinks about how work can also meet their higher-level needs. When a manager does this, employees feel their higher levels of motivation.

If you think of a job only in terms of lower-level needs, then your employees aren't likely to become highly motivated. But if you pay them appropriately and give them more authority and responsibility over their work, they'll find greater motivation—because their work will be meeting higher-level needs.

Then don't forget to act on their suggestions.

- Acknowledge that everyone is unique. Inquire about a person's special talents and skills. You might uncover a diamond in the rough.

- Send out an employee survey about attitudes in the workplace and their suggestions for improvements. Don't ignore the results. Use the findings to make changes that will improve everyone's working conditions, including yours.

- Conduct exit interviews with employees who leave voluntarily. Use what you learn to create a work environment that people won't want to leave.

GTHOOYO!   SMART

GTHOOYO! No, that's not a sneeze, just a few words of advice—Get The Heck Out Of Your Office! Wander   MANAGING
around. Spend time with your employees. If that's unusual, it may be difficult at first, since they may suspect you of spying or trying to infiltrate their ranks. But when they realize you're not the enemy, you can really get to know employees as people, what they need from you to perform well, and how you can better work together to fulfill your mutual goals.

- Assume that personal growth and recognition, creativity, and meaningful work are as important to your workers as they are to you. Ask employees to describe their ideal job and what they like or don't like about their work. Use what you learn to make work more fulfilling.

After you've identified the needs of your employees and gained a sense of how their work activities and environments allow them to meet

FEAR AND SUSPICION

When you're surveying employees about their problems on the job and ways to improve the working environment, it's important that they believe you're honestly interested in what they have to say. They need to be sure you're not going to use what you learn against them because they're complaining. A good way to do this is to start with groups, listen to what they have to say, and then quickly make changes they suggest. They'll learn that you want to make improvements and you want their help to do so.

those needs, what do you do? That depends on what you've learned. Consider the following suggestions.

How to meet *physiological needs* at work:

- Create a comfortable, safe, and pleasant environment for employees. Show them that they don't need to park their personalities outside the door.
- Pay competitive salaries so that employees can comfortably provide for themselves and their families.
- Provide greater financial opportunities for employees who want or need more money—such as overtime or other incentives.

How to meet *security and safety needs* at work:

- Be consistent and fair with everyone.
- Protect employees with safety rules and policies.
- Take extra steps to protect workers against violent crimes. Hire security.
- Communicate information regularly.

How to meet *social needs* at work:

- Give employees opportunities to work in groups and with other departments.
- Create opportunities to help employees develop relationships and become accepted and appreciated by teammates.
- Show your concern for team members and encourage them to do likewise.

How to meet *ego-status needs* at work:

- Give positive feedback and praise on a regular basis.

- Let people excel and move into areas of responsibility that are high-profile and that demonstrate their talents and skills.
- Set up different levels of recognition programs based on levels of performance.
- Ask for people's opinions. Involve others in the planning process.
- Always say "Thank you."

How to meet *self-actualization needs* at work:
- Allow autonomy.
- Give employees the freedom to be creative.
- Treat mistakes as learning experiences.
- Provide opportunities for more challenging work.
- Support personal and professional growth through ongoing learning and training opportunities.

You can't help every employee meet every need, of course. That's impossible—and there are certain dangers in expecting our work, no matter how satisfying, to constitute our entire life. But if you take certain steps to help your employees meet some of their needs in their work, and to find greater motivation in what they do in the organizational community, then you make it much easier for them to do the rest. You also make it easier to do your own job, because you don't need to run around with the whip of fear or a carrot dangling from a stick.

Human Nature at Work

The title of this chapter is "Working with Human Nature"—and for good reason. When we're at work, we can't turn off our human nature. Our needs don't change when we walk through the workplace door. To get people to perform at high levels, you must plug into their nature, affirm them, and help them meet their own needs. You have to make work a place where employees feel good about themselves and where the work helps employees meet their personal needs. When you do that, employees will naturally come to understand that doing well by the company is how they do well by themselves.

Managers—Nurture–Nature—What We Give Attention to Flourishes; What We Ignore Dies

Employee-engagement expert, author, and former corporate chief-of-staff Scott Carbonara believes that both *nature and human nature* can best be understood from a behavioral viewpoint. Carbonara relies on his background as an award-winning behavioral therapist. He quotes the words of American statesman Robert Green Ingersoll who said, "In nature there are neither rewards nor punishments; there are consequences."

The Houseplant Concept for Employee Motivation

Have you ever needed to rotate a houseplant because it started leaning too far toward the window? Did you ever consider who taught the plant to grow toward the sunlight? Plants don't need to be taught to use solar energy for photosynthesis—the process to convert carbon dioxide into organic compounds. The plant doesn't receive a reward or punishment from the sunlight. The plant receives a consequence. When the plant gets adequate sunlight, it thrives; when a plant gets too much or too little sunlight, it struggles.

Carbonara explains that people are not so different from plants. "I start with a simple premise," he says. "People tend to do what they do because they get what they want when they do it."

Carbonara suggests that when appropriate work behaviors like completing tasks on time, producing high-quality results, providing outstanding customer service, etc., are not happening regularly, the leader might look at two areas. First, does the work environment provide positive reinforcement for doing what is expected? In addition to pay and benefits, positive reinforcement can come from the work itself, coworker praise, or the recognition from someone whose words matter to the employee. Second, does the work environment unintentionally provide punishment for doing what's expected? For example, does the person who completes her work early get assigned more work? Does someone who is performing at a lower standard make more money?

Show 'Em the Money, But Don't Stop There

"I always recommend that leaders answer this question: *What happens to an employee at work when he or she does what is expected?* Many leaders say, 'I pay them!' But pay is a given. In order for people to willingly go above and beyond what's expected, they have to want to do it," Carbonara states. He in fact addressed a major attrition problem by focusing beyond the pay scale, as he learned that the true reason employees were quitting was not because they weren't happy with their salaries, but because they weren't happy with the work environment.

Leaders who believe that a paycheck is the only form of positive reinforcement may not fully understand this concept. Positive reinforcement can be a "consequence" that follows a behavior—ensuring that the behavior will happen again. "You can tell that you've delivered positive reinforcement if the performer gets what he likes and wants, and then he is happy to repeat the behavior that earned him the reward," Carbonara explains.

On the other hand, Carbonara explains: "If you don't see the right behaviors occurring, you haven't yet found something an employee finds reinforcing. So keep looking."

Provide More Sunlight

The simplest way for leaders to increase the amount of positive reinforcement that leads to engaged employees is to provide *more sunlight!* Look around nature for examples:

- A spider spins webs in locations where they will not be torn down, but also where they will have a ready supply of food.
- A bird will seek protection from a rain shower, but also take advantage of the worms that come to the surface.
- A squirrel will hover around the base of an oak tree so it has a quick escape from predators, but also a large supply of acorns.

Likewise, Carbonara suggests that you look around your office to find out what excites your employees: An employee who socializes frequently may wish to avoid feeling isolated, but may be rewarded by being given collaborative work assignments. An employee who gets his work done on time or early may not like the feeling of falling behind schedule, but he may be thrilled at the chance to be given additional or more challenging responsibilities. An employee whose peers come to her for answers may be in a role that is no longer challenging, but she might accomplish even more if given the chance to be an employee coach or mentor.

Know Your People

Carbonara stresses that a behavioral approach doesn't run contrary to Theory X/Theory Y. A behavioral approach simply challenges leaders to suppress their own Theory X/Theory Y beliefs and get to know what engages their employees.

"There's no one-size-fits-all when it comes to what people find rewarding or reinforcing," Carbonara points out. "One employee may love public praise, another may despise it. Know what your employees crave—attention, tangible items, increased opportunities or exposure, training, etc.—and then give those things to them when they do what you need them to accomplish."

SMART   **KYP STRATEGY**

MANAGING

Carbonara suggests implementing the KYP strategy, or "Know Your People." Knowing them means more than just knowing what motivates them at work, but also knowing them as human beings. He once saw a diabetic employee "rewarded" for her efforts by being given a gift of chocolate. That's not smart management! Employees are engaged when they have at least one friend at work. Be that friend who knows your people!

Gossip Only About the Good Stuff

Carbonara concedes, though, that there does seem to be one behavior that employees find universally disengaging when it comes from a leader: gossip. "If you want to lose your effectiveness and lower your engagement levels overnight, become known for gossiping about and bad-mouthing your employees," Carbonara states, using employee engagement survey data from a multi-million-dollar healthcare organization he worked with for many years.

"Here's what I suggest to leaders as a behavior that most employees link to their own engagement: giving praises behind their back," Carbonara says. "Whereas gossip tears down trust and destroys morale, having a coworker tell you, 'The boss told me that no one knows more about _____.'"

Manager's Checklist for Chapter 2

☑ Understand human nature and why people behave as they do. That way, you can better relate to your employees and build a more productive and enjoyable work environment.

☑ Managers view employees according to different assumptions about human nature. Two extremes are presented in the concept of Theory X and Theory Y developed by Douglas McGregor. Theory X assumes employees don't like to work and must be carefully supervised. Theory Y assumes people like to work and want the opportunity and support that will allow them to perform at high levels.

☑ People act according to basic needs. Abraham Maslow studied those needs and arranged them into several levels according to their importance in motivating us, from the most fundamental physiological and security needs, to needs for association with others, to needs for ego gratification, to the highest level need for self-actualization. Know what drives each of your employees so that you can link job activities with each individual's personal needs and help him or her find greater motivation to perform well.

☑ Check out Gallup's Q12 Research on Employee Engagement at Gallup.com

☑ Try Scott Carbonara's houseplant "Be the Light" concept for employee motivation that survives and thrives. Visit ScottCarbonara.com.

Encouraging Entrepreneurial Thinking

Help People Feel Like They Own the Place

If you want your employees to be motivated to do their best, and if you want them to be the most valuable asset on your balance sheet, then let them feel and experience ownership in the organization. Effective managers make every employee feel like a business partner. Why? Because when people feel ownership of something, they look out for it.

Make Everyone Feel Like a Business Partner

Encouraging an *entrepreneurial mind-set* goes beyond profit sharing and stock options. It's a motivating attitude instilled in others by you, the manager. We see this attitude demonstrated and translated into profits in companies such as Zappos, Google, 3M, Southwest Airlines, Nordstrom, Intel, Starbucks, Walmart, Microsoft, Pixar, Netflix, Johnson & Johnson, SAS, LinkedIn, USAA, and hundreds of smaller companies, where employees are motivated to take exceptional pride in their work because they're treated like business partners and not hired help.

How do you create such an atmosphere of entrepreneurial attitude and pride? You begin by understanding and acknowledging that employees today want a say in how the organization is being run. Their input can be extremely powerful, especially if they know and understand how the

KEY TERM

Entrepreneurial mind-set As it's used here, I mean "thinking like a business owner." Although the term can be used to characterize somebody who acts independently, perhaps even as a maverick, it's intended here to convey a sense of feeling joint ownership, of being a partner in a business, and caring about the success of that business.

organization operates. By the way you interact with employees, you can help them begin thinking as entrepreneurs and feel more accountable for the organization meeting its goals.

To succeed in today's rapidly changing work environment, employees need to know far more about the organization than just how to do their specific jobs. So you must help workers better understand the entire organization, gain a clearer perspective of how the organization operates, learn what the competition is doing, and develop the ability to take intelligent risks and be creative. In other words, you need to help employees take full advantage of their human capabilities to perform at high levels.

Five Steps to Creating Entrepreneurial Thinkers

There are five steps you as a manager can take to help your employees think and act more like entrepreneurs on the job:

1. Explain the organization.
2. Demonstrate how the organization operates and generates income.
3. Help your employees understand the competition.
4. Encourage intelligent risk-taking.
5. Inspire innovative thinking.

In implementing these strategies, remember that you're not trying to create a bunch of independent decision makers who don't take into consideration the needs of their colleagues or the organization. You're simply trying to help your employees feel a sense of ownership and pride in their work and a sense of commitment to the organization and its goals.

Step 1. Explain the Organization

One key to your success as a manager is that you understand the organization's mission, its goals, and its strategies for achieving these goals. If you're a manager, you know how much it helps to see the big picture within which your specific responsibilities lie. Because you understand how you fit into the organization, you better understand your role and why the company values your contribution. It's easier to identify with the company and feel motivated to work harder and smarter.

It's the same for your employees. If they understand about the organization and their role in it, they can feel similarly motivated and more likely to develop a positive attitude toward their jobs and their fellow employees. You don't need to make everyone managers, of course. But you can help your employees better understand what's going on beyond their desks, cubicles, and work stations and outside the walls of your department. When they know how they fit in and the difference they make, they can do their work more intelligently.

How can you help your employees become more aware of their role and feel more a part of what's happening throughout the organization? Here are a few suggestions for you to consider:

■ Give employees books and articles about the organization. Keep a scrapbook to record important chapters in the organization's history—the bad as well as the good. This will give employees a historical perspective of the company and inspire in them a greater sense of identity and pride.

■ Show employees how to understand and interpret the organization's annual report, if the organization issues one. Point out the CEO's message, which can be valuable in clarifying the organization's mission, measuring progress toward long-term goals, and describing challenges the organization might face in the future.

■ Share the monthly departmental profit-and-loss statement with employees. This will help them understand even better how their work fits into their small section of the organization, their neighborhood of your economic community.

■ Help employees understand the organization's mission statement. Look for opportunities to discuss the mission statement with members of your team. Show how it drives behavior and decisions in the organization.

■ Encourage employees to identify things they can do to contribute directly to achieving the organization's mission statement objectives.

Discuss with employees the role(s) of your department and whatever strategic goals you might have. Then give them the chance to act on their ideas.

■ Encourage employees to tackle obstacles by having them lead task forces to find solutions and implement them. This can be as formal or informal as you deem appropriate. What's essential is to encourage your employees to think together about how they can improve their work environment and the performance of your department.

■ Reinforce the value of your organization's communications department, if you have one. Suggest that employees contact the department for copies of executive briefings, recent newspaper clippings that profile or discuss the organization, recent ad campaigns, and corporate brochures. Or, simply get copies of these documents yourself and post them around your department.

Zappos took this a step further and asked each employee to serve as author of these materials. That is, each employee was asked to submit an answer to the following question: "If you had to describe your company's culture in two or three paragraphs, what would you say? If you asked your coworkers to do the same, how similar (or different) do you think their answers would be?" Then, Zappos took all the answers, unchanged, and compiled them into a Culture Book so that new hires could learn about the company culture, issues, concerns, and strengths firsthand. Not only did this give employees ownership in communicating their experiences—and new hires a means of getting to the true story quickly—it also gave managers key information on how to improve their leadership. Indirectly, it served as great public relations, as outside groups have actually requested to read the Culture Book!

With self-publishing being so simple these days, any organization can create such a book for their employees. Jocelyn Godfrey, editor and owner of Spiritus Communications, Inc., a marketing and publishing consulting firm, states, "Every employee and organization has a story. Putting this story into writing in the form of a book will document it, make it come alive with breath and color, and allow you to 'edit' your corporate plan and culture as you progress. If the thought of writing a corporate book overwhelms you, find a professional editor to oversee the project and make it easy to deliver."

Step 2. Demonstrate How the Organization Operates and Generates Income

As a manager, you understand how your organization operates and manages its finances. So you might not realize what it's like to work without knowing how every person and every job affects the bottom line. When employees become aware of how the organization runs and how it spends and brings in money, they become more motivated to help make a difference.

How can you help each of your employees understand how he or she alone impacts the organization's bottom line? Here are a few recommendations:

- Arrange for a business basics training program for all employees. There are several on the market that can be customized to your organization's needs. These programs may use a game format to explain how your organization operates and how it makes and loses money. This can be an enjoyable way to teach employees the business. With the advance in technology, employees can now affordably watch webinars or dial into teleseminars remotely at a convenient time, and learn about almost any aspect of the business process.

- Give employees documents that describe strategic plans, financial goals, and operating philosophies of the organization. Again, the corporate communications office may have just what you need. You might want to explain a few of these documents at every departmental meeting. There's no need to turn your meeting into a seminar; just take a few minutes to sum up each document and why it matters to the organization and your employees. Then, summarize the impact of your group in all this, in terms of costs and income generated.

- Analyze scenarios that show the impact one person has on the entire organization. This can be a real eye-opener! Jack Stack's *The Great Game of Business* offers some good suggestions on how to do this.

You can probably come up with scenarios for your organization. In fact, most organizations have horror stories involving employees who didn't care enough about a particular job or didn't fully understand the importance of what they were expected to do. Whether you find actual examples

---

OPEN-BOOK MANAGING

TOOLS

Over the past decade, the idea of open-book management has become popular. This concept involves sharing the organization's financial data with employees and showing them specifically what they cost and what value they add to the organization. A good resource for learning about this approach is the influential book, *The Great Game of Business*, by Jack Stack. Information is also available on the Internet at www.greatgame.com.

Zappos is also known for implementing open-book management. Founder Tony Hsieh has sent detailed and candid messages to employees, even during financial distress. In this way, he allowed employees to create a more profit-minded business. At one point in Zappos' history, Hsieh even allowed employees to propose solutions for helping the bottom line—such as cutting their own hours in exchange for pay cuts. In doing so, he was able to save Zappos from pending demise, and drive them to exceed their $1 billion gross sales goal several years ahead of schedule.

---

or create realistic scenarios, the point is to help your employees see how one person's attitude and behavior might directly impact the organization's bottom line, potential pay raises, bonuses, profit sharing, and so on.

When you help your employees think in terms of the big picture and understand the domino effect of every action they take, you begin to instill in them an entrepreneurial mind-set that creates a winning and motivated organization. Of course, in some organizations, because of the attitude of management, this might also instill fear in employees. But the whole point of this book is to help you move away from that approach. You don't want to create fearful employees. You want to develop smart, skilled, and highly motivated employees who understand their role in helping the organization succeed.

Step 3. Help Your Employees Understand the Competition

When employees pull together to compete in the marketplace, their level of motivation rises when they understand just who and what they are competing against. Nothing brings a team together in tighter cooperation than the challenge of performing at higher and higher levels than its competitors, helping the organization to grow as a result.

You don't necessarily need to take a "rah-rah-rah" attitude, as if organizations were high school football teams. This is just another way to

THE IMPACT OF AN EMPLOYEE

Let's assume a baggage handler for an airline isn't very motivated to do his job. How does his performance affect the organization?

A flight arrives late and a passenger's briefcase must be transferred to another flight within minutes. The baggage handler doesn't feel like hustling the briefcase to the other flight. He thinks, "What's in it for me?" So he leaves the case on the ramp until the next flight to that city departs—six hours later.

The passenger waiting for the briefcase has an important meeting that evening and needs some materials from the briefcase. She complains to a customer service rep for the airline, who explains that the briefcase will be arriving later, although not in time for the meeting. As a result, the irate frequent flier shares her dismay with other passengers and then later with her colleagues at the meeting, when she cannot provide the necessary materials to help her company land the big account.

What's the impact of the baggage handler on the airline's bottom line? The airline lost a valuable customer and perhaps all of her company's future business. It also probably lost a few of the other passengers and some of the customer's business associates. That means a significant loss in revenue, possibly tens of thousands of dollars, especially as the story ripples out even further—it also means more work for other employees, to make up for the negligence of that one baggage handler.

Multiply this impact by the number of incidents that might occur throughout this airline in a given year. Now we're talking about hundreds of thousands of dollars in lost revenue and a lot of extra effort and expense.

help employees understand the big picture, because your competitors are part of that picture.

You can learn a lot from the competition—not just how to win a greater market share, but how to improve your organization. In that spirit, here are some ways for you and your employees to learn more about your competitors:

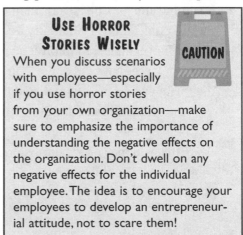

USE HORROR STORIES WISELY

CAUTION

When you discuss scenarios with employees—especially if you use horror stories from your own organization—make sure to emphasize the importance of understanding the negative effects on the organization. Don't dwell on any negative effects for the individual employee. The idea is to encourage your employees to develop an entrepreneurial attitude, not to scare them!

- Encourage employees to ask customers to evaluate how your organization measures up to the competition.

- Put someone in charge of obtaining the competition's promotional literature, so that you can all learn more about their products or services.
- Start a file of *competitor profiles*. These profiles can help your team develop strategies for gaining competitive advantage.

Just as it's important for your employees to know about your competitors, it's also important for your employees to know more about your industry. After all, if employees can become more motivated by understanding the impact of their presence in the organization, they can also be inspired by knowing your organization's impact in its industry.

KEY TERM — **Competitor Profile** A document that includes information about competitor pricing, copies of advertisements, an annual report, profiles of top executives, a list of strengths and weaknesses, philosophies and values, awards and recognition received, market share and global reach, and recruiting policies and employee incentive plans.

How can you help your employees learn more about your industry? The following suggestions—some of which may seem quite ambitious—will give you some ideas:

- Allow employees to stay current with industry changes and meet industry movers and shakers by sending them to conferences and trade shows.
- Go online and look up government documents relevant to the industry and publications by industry associations.
- Budget for membership in professional associations. Then make sure your employees have the opportunity to read association publications. You might even want to e-mail and tweet an occasional link to an article from an association ezine or e-journal, especially industry overviews and best practices case studies. (If you e-mail the whole article, be aware that you may need permission from the publisher to do so.)
- Look for books, publications, and research information on the Internet that cover practices and trends in industry categories related to your own.
- Join Internet discussion groups on subjects dealing with your industry or management in general. (To find out some that deal with man-

agement, check this Internet site: www.quality.org, or do a search on LinkedIn or Facebook to find pertinent groups and join discussions.)

- Join associations or encourage your organization to do so based on common denominators, such as type of business or industry, organization size and ranking, market niche, and so on.

Implement a company-wide e-newsletter or Facebook page where you can provide updates and tips to employees in an easy-to-follow and engaging format. Encourage dialogue.

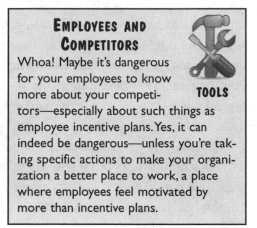

EMPLOYEES AND COMPETITORS

TOOLS

Whoa! Maybe it's dangerous for your employees to know more about your competitors—especially about such things as employee incentive plans. Yes, it can indeed be dangerous—unless you're taking specific actions to make your organization a better place to work, a place where employees feel motivated by more than incentive plans.

Remember: your purpose in following any of these suggestions is to help your employees become more motivated by helping them understand the significance of what they and your organization are doing. So be sensitive to their needs and feelings and attentive to the dangers of trying to do too much. Some of your employees might feel overwhelmed by information and intimidated by perceived expectations. Your purpose is to allow them to explore their horizons, not to run them into the ground! Be sure you tell them as much.

Step 4. Encourage Intelligent Risk-Taking

Risk has long been considered a four-letter word for success. But creative and calculated risk-taking can improve any organization. That means that management should help employees try new ways to do their work, experiment to make improvements, and encourage and support them in taking those risks.

Why aren't more employees willing to take risks? Probably because the few times they tried to and things went wrong, they were either fired or severely disciplined. Even when employees succeed at something risky, with a pat on the back for the result, they may also get chastised for taking the initiative. After all, there are channels and chains of command, assigned responsibilities, managers paid to take risks, and so on and so forth. Even in more recent decades, management has sent out a mixed message: *We want you to feel empowered and take risks—just don't screw up!*

Everyone makes mistakes. Thomas Edison is famous for saying during the process to find a filament that would work in his invention of the light bulb, "I have not failed. I've just found 10,000 things that won't work." Good managers know that failure is an integral part of success, and they also recognize that developing a risk-taking mentality is part of helping employees develop an entrepreneurial approach in their work. So you must support, encourage, and reward intelligent risk-taking in the organization. After all, the only way to get better is to try new things. Organizations that don't innovate stagnate—and may go out of business.

As Geoff Colvin points out in *Talent Is Overrated*, managers at Google well understand that their success as an organization relies on their employees. Google knows a thing or two about how to hire the best employees. More than that, they know how to keep them, and they know how to keep them happy. Perhaps the success in their hiring is how Google has used around $5 billion of its capital while creating nearly $124 billion in shareholder wealth.

Not surprisingly, innovative companies like 3M and Google allow employees to spend up to 20 percent of their time on any project that they find interesting. Remember 3M? One researcher became interested in making an adhesive that turned out to lack the right stickiness for glue. But that little side project of his was the origin of Post-It® Notes. It's a good bet that 3M leaders were happy they let employees experiment and tinker with pet projects.

How can you build a culture in which your employees feel comfortable taking risks? Well, you can't do it by words alone, as many managers have tried—unsuccessfully. The following suggestions are a good starting point:

- Allow your employees to make decisions that involve risks.
- Treat mistakes as "teachable moments." When things don't work out, recognize and take advantage of the opportunity to help employees learn something.

Take Shots

SMART

"You miss 100 percent of the shots you don't take." These are the words of hockey great Wayne Gretzky—and they should be posted prominently on every wall around your workplace. This attitude has helped Gretzky earn the nickname "The Great One." **MANAGING** It's important to note that Gretzky has won awards not only for scoring goals, but also for assists—for helping his teammates score.

Similarly, Michelangelo stated, "The greater danger for most of us lies not in setting our aim too high and falling short; but in setting our aim too low, and achieving our mark." See how many great achievers were willing to fail?

- Expect setbacks as a natural result of people taking risks.
- Encourage initiative and celebrate successes that come from employees taking initiative. If things don't turn out well, praise employees anyway and ask, "What can we learn here so we can do better next time?"
- Help employees understand the difference between healthy risks and foolish chances. (And remember that the difference isn't necessarily black-and-white or accepted as such by everyone.)
- Set an example. Try new things. If you never falter, it shows you're probably playing it safe and not trying new things yourself. If you hesitate to take risks, why should your employees feel free to take risks?
- Demonstrate how to evaluate whether to take a risk. For example, look at the critical issues, assess opportunities against objective criteria to determine the potential return, then decide whether the risk is worth it, and if the organization can stand behind whatever results.

Step 5. Inspire Innovative Thinking

When organizations survive and thrive, it's generally because managers know how to change with their situations—and sometimes keep ahead of the changes around them. Especially during the financial hard times that many companies have endured in the recent past, resilience and an ability to think on one's feet are crucial. Companies have greater odds for success when managers allow or even encourage innovative thinking among their employees. That means managers need to help their employees feel motivated to try different things.

How can you inspire your employees to think in new ways and encourage them to innovate on the job? Here are a few techniques to guide you:

- Set aside special time to brainstorm with employees and investigate innovative and creative new ideas.
- Support innovative ideas and help implement them.
- Set up a seminar on how to think creatively and/or make available books on this subject, such as *A Whack on the Side of the Head* by Roger Von Oech, *Thinkertoys* by Michael Michalko, *Now Discover Your Strengths* by Marcus Buckingham, or the Briefcase Books title, *Manager's Guide to Fostering Innovation and Creativity in Teams* by Charles Prather.

INTELLIGENT RISK TAKING

What's the difference between "good risks" and "foolish chances"? Sure, we can all agree on some extreme cases. But let's consider something more problematic—a lottery, for example. Would you risk a dollar to win $10,000 if the odds were 3-to-1? How about 30-to-1? What if they were 30,000-to-1? At what point does the gamble go from a good risk to a foolish chance? We're not likely to agree on a specific point. Keep that in mind when you talk with your employees about taking risks: they may be unclear about what's good and what's bad. Provide some examples to help them understand.

- Tell everyone in the organization about the creative ideas of their co-workers, through special announcements, e-mail, e-blasts, e-letters, Skype, in conversations, and organizational publications.
- Use music to inspire creative energy.

You may be thinking, "All of this makes sense, but it won't work in my department." Well, maybe you're right—but *why not?* What keeps your people from thinking creatively? If you believe your company is not suited for creativity, think of examples like Red Hat, a growing open source software company consistently ranked highly as a "Best Place to Work." Who would think that a technology company would need to reward creativity? Red Hat does. In fact, they make a point to hire creative people who have worked as filmmakers, writers, and so on, even if they also rely on them for their technical drill-down skills. They also foster sto-

> **EVALUATING RISK**
>
> TRICKS OF THE TRADE
>
> There's no way to eliminate risk, but there are good methods for evaluating it. This checklist can help you determine whether a risk is worth taking:
>
> 1. Examine the critical issues.
> 2. Assess the opportunity against objective criteria to determine the potential return.
> 3. Ask yourself if the risk seems worth it.
> 4. Confirm that the organization will stand behind the end results.

rytelling as part of their internal communication process and aim to tie employees to the corporate vision in this way.

If you believe there are obstacles to fostering creativity, it's up to you to identify them and do something about removing them. Maybe money is your obstacle. Michael Michalowicz, author of *The Toilet Paper Entrepreneur*, talks about how he was able to build two multimillion-dollar businesses without having deep pockets or exceptional media skills. Whatever obstacles you see, how you deconstruct them for your employees depends, of course, on your particular environment. But here are a few general suggestions:

- Show faith in your employees' capabilities by empowering them to try new ways of doing tasks and providing the resources they need to do this. If you don't have faith in your people, you send the message that innovation is not welcome.
- Address and eliminate fears employees have about creative thinking. Some people, for example, don't think they're capable of being creative. Others tend to always focus on matters of practicality: they analyze and judge ideas as quickly as they arise.
- Make sure everyone understands the basic principle of *brainstorming*—to provide a free and open environment that encourages and inspires everyone to offer whatever ideas may occur to him or her—no matter how "impractical" they may seem at first.
- Regularly emphasize the positive aspects of innovative solutions—and the disadvantages of always doing the same things in the same ways.
- Never penalize someone for trying something new that ends up being a mistake. Encourage learning from the experience instead.

- Encourage freedom of expression and unique thinking.
- Don't assume something won't work just because nobody's tried it.
- Suspend critical judgment when someone presents an idea. Talk about how

> **KEY TERM** **Brainstorming** This term has been used so often and in so many ways that it deserves a few words here. The principle behind brainstorming is to create an open environment for offering lots of ideas, without any thought about how practical they might be—or about who should get credit for them.

you can work together to make it work, not what's wrong with it.
- Loosen up and lighten up. Don't take yourself too seriously.

Help Your Employees Feel As If They Own the Business

If you want your employees to put more of themselves into their work, help them find more of themselves in it. That was the basic message in the first two chapters of this book. This third chapter has taken us a little further into entrepreneurial thinking.

This is likely to be just a small step for your employees, at least in theory, because people who do a job typically want to feel like it's more than a job and like they're more than just part of a machine. For you, on the other hand, this step may be a little more difficult.

Keep in mind, then, this basic idea: if you want your employees to be motivated to do their best, help them feel as if they control their jobs, as if they belong to a community, and—most of all—as if they own the business.

> **TRICKS OF THE TRADE**
>
> ### A Brainstorming Session
>
> Facilitating a good brainstorming session is easiest if you keep it simple. Borrow an employee from outside your department—someone who can think fast and write even faster. Get a marking pen and a flip chart or chalk and a blackboard. Then have that person serve as a scribe, simply getting every idea down. Having a scribe allows your employees to "go with the flow," and having the ideas accumulate openly usually encourages the flow. Plus, the faster the flow, the less time people have to focus on any of the ideas and start thinking about practicalities.

COLORED FLAGS

Sometimes when we try to hold "idea" meetings, we tend to do too much at once—and end up doing too little well. That's when it might help to use flags.

Make three flags—green, yellow, and red. (Use colored paper and pencils to keep it simple.) Bring the flags to your next meeting and explain their meaning: green means we offer ideas freely, yellow means we explore those ideas, and red means we look for potential problems. When you want to encourage employees to offer ideas, simply post the green flag in a prominent place, such as the center of the table. This reminds everyone to brainstorm freely. When you want to shift to examining the suggested ideas, replace the green flag with the yellow one. For the final phase, post the red flag to remind everyone to focus on critically examining the ideas.

Engaging Remote Employees to Act as Entrepreneurs

In this high-tech galaxy, more employees than ever before are working remotely. Whether taking a work day at home to tend to a sick child, checking in from a beach café while on a working vacation, or contracting for a company to fulfill a specific need, more people than ever are logging in from an office that's often closer to their home than a central office. This new way of working, without close supervision, means that employee management and motivation need to take a different approach.

Jocelyn Godfrey, owner of Spiritus Communications, Inc.—a marketing and publishing consulting company for speakers, authors, and entrepreneurs—states: "Working remotely has unique advantages, in that the hiring pool ends up more like a hiring ocean. Suddenly, instead of being limited to your hometown, you can find employees as far away as you can imagine, and connect via Skype, e-mail, Facebook, and more, to manage projects. You can hire people for as few or as many hours as you need and hand select the best person for the best job—or manage

REMOTE MOTIVATION   SMART

Working remotely can make employees want to take a snooze or can empower them to want to please you even more. Manage wisely, by issuing clear expectations, implementing systems, staying in the loop, and praising and rewarding good efforts and outcomes. Find out what motivates each remote employee so that you can tailor your reinforcement to his or her style.

MANAGING

staff who come in only occasionally. But ... if you want to meet your goals, you must keep each project managed, and each employee engaged—just as if you were all under the same roof."

To do this, Godfrey recommends empowering remote employees to think and act like they are entrepreneurs.

Keeping Remote Employees Engaged

Here are Godfrey's recommendations for keeping remote people productive and motivated:

1. Get to know remote employees, just like you would those in your office. Help them get to know each other. You can't meet for coffee before work, but you can spend five minutes asking about someone's weekend, kids' baseball camp, crazy oversized dogs, ski jumping habit, or wild wisteria vine. In addition, find out their work experience and goals, and introduce them to other colleagues who may benefit them. You can send e-mails, cc:ing other team members, to introduce remote staff to one another. Friend each other on Facebook if it feels appropriate. If you build trust and rapport with your remote employees, and help them feel at ease with each other, they are bound to be more bonded to you and your vision, and more apt to stay loyal.

2. Provide context. If you are starting a new project, inform all employees of the bigger picture. Godfrey hires designers, web programmers, printers, and more, and lets them all know who the project is being done for, and what it aims to accomplish on a broader scale. Designing a logo may hold much more meaning when it is being done for a campaign to end hunger—especially for a nonprofit president who is about to appear on *The Today Show*—than it would if people were only working on their part of the project and didn't have an opportunity to see how they fit in with the entire process.

3. Implement tools to keep tasks organized. Godfrey suggests using a project management site like Basecamp to keep to-dos organized, assigned, and dated. This also allows employees to track progress, and check projects off the to-do list (which is always satisfying!). Conduct weekly meetings through a conference line wherein everyone can join. Send out group e-mails with updates afterwards outlining the key points, addressing problem areas, offering solutions, and thanking everyone for joining.

4. Stay humble. Ask for feedback. Just because you have more years of experience in a given field doesn't mean that you might not run across a remote employee who can teach you something. "I always approach each contractor or remote employee as an expert in his or her field," says Godfrey. "I clearly state what I would like the person to do, how I think it can be done, and then make it clear that I would love any comments, suggestions, or questions. This paves the way for process improvement and keeps employees feeling like they are entrepreneurs in my business."

5. Celebrate commitment, milestones, completed jobs, and successes. This may mean sending an inspirational quote or word to people in the midst of a hard project to remind them that they're not alone. Or it may mean issuing praise for something that was unveiled or accomplished. If the people working are freelancers, pay them on time, let them know you appreciate them, recommend them to others, and hire them again! *Do not* skip this step, or these people may become discouraged, resentful, and less likely to want to work with your company when you need them in the future. In other words, by celebrating successes, you enhance motivation, and by ignoring this step, you undermine it.

6. Commit to stay away from the drama. Without the social barriers that exist in person, it's all too easy with remote employees to hit send on an e-mail blasting the CEO; but don't do it. If there is a problem with a staff member or superior, address it internally—but don't share your misgivings electronically unless you want them to potentially go viral to everyone's dismay, especially your own.

If you do keep remote employees engaged, Godfrey suggests, these employees will become not only your friends and future colleagues, but also the ones who recommend your services to others, thus marketing your business.

The Doctor Is in

I found out earlier this year that there might be a fast cure for many of my clients' employee ailments. And to my surprise it all came in one pill—no, not a medicine you'd get from the drugstore but another kind of medicine. The kind you get from a motivational business growth expert, like Ken Wright, in his book, *The People Pill*.

I have recommended Ken's book to all the managers I work with and have sent them straightaway to Ken's website: www.Engage4Results.com.

Everything about Ken's book and his site is motivating and how-to, results-oriented.

Did You Know?

According to Ken Wright's research:

- Over 70 percent of American employees do not feel engaged in their work.
- A meager 18 percent of Australians believe they are engaged at work (Ken's an Aussie).
- Disengagement costs the U.S. economy $328 billion per year!
- Over 90 percent of American employees leave their jobs, as they fail to make an emotional connection with their bosses. And only 33 percent of America's employees view their managers as strong leaders.

So what's the remedy?

Prescription: *The People Pill*

"The first step is to develop your people specifically to maximize their potential," stresses Wright. "All of my company's proprietary programs are employee generated. When employees are proud of themselves and their performance, they work at a consistently higher capacity and are more motivated and satisfied at their job. They also stay at the company longer because they are engaged!"

According to Wright, employees' engagement in

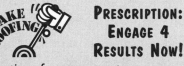

PRESCRIPTION: ENGAGE 4 RESULTS NOW!

Questions for managers to answer:

- Are your employees fully invested in your organization?
- Do your people see their leaders as solid and respected?
- How can you prevent low employee engagement in your workplace?

Accelerate workplace performance to its optimum level. Visit www.Engage4 Results.com today and get lots of tips, tools, and ideas to kick motivation and employee engagement up a full notch.

their work will translate into positive interactions with your company's clients and customers, too, resulting in exceptional customer care, service and engendering powerful customer loyalty. This inevitably transforms into larger profits for your company, emphasizes Wright. "A leader needs to focus on feelings and building confidence. The latest neuroscience research tells us that the sheer belief that you can achieve something is more important than skills and abilities. Personally, I like the quote by Carl Buechner, says Wright, 'People will forget what you do, forget what you say, but they will never forget how you make them feel.'"

Manager's Checklist for Chapter 3

☑ It's important to encourage entrepreneurial thinking because people who feel ownership of something tend to care more about it.

☑ To get your employees to feel and act more like entrepreneurs, explain the organization to them, show them how it works and manages its finances, help them understand the competition, encourage them to take intelligent risks, and inspire innovative thinking.

☑ Help your employees better understand the organization and their role in it, so they can feel more motivated in their work and develop a more positive attitude toward their jobs and their fellow employees.

☑ Implement Jocelyn Godfrey's six tips for keeping remote employees engaged. Visit SpiritusCommunications.com for more tips and tools in this area and others.

☑ When organizations thrive, it's generally because the managers encourage their employees to think, to try to do different things, and to do things differently.

Linking Motivation to Performance

Help Employees to Touch Their Potential

If you occasionally feel as though you're having little or no impact on the motivation of your employees, you're not alone.

Let's face it: you can't always change or control certain factors that affect your employees' enthusiasm for their jobs. Some things—such as working conditions, specific assignments, salaries and benefits you can provide, or even factors not related to work—are simply out of your control at times.

Still it's important to remember that there's a link between motivation and performance. Employees work harder and smarter not for you but for themselves. We need our employees to make a connection between meeting their own needs and doing exceptional work. That's where management comes in.

In meeting the challenge of linking motivation and performance, don't yield to the temptation to pull out the whip and the carrot on a stick. Yes, the challenge may seem difficult, but you can overcome it. The key is to learn the techniques that work for other managers and then try them when they seem appropriate. See what works for you and what doesn't. Commit to a general strategy, so your employees don't regard these techniques as simply a "flavor of the week" series of gimmicks. Understand why the techniques we describe here work, then try those that you think might help you more effectively influence what your employees are motivated to do.

This chapter covers many of the techniques you can use. You'll find some specific strategies that work well. But the intent is also to inspire you to think "outside the box" of traditional management styles and approaches that you or your fellow managers have been using. You might be surprised at how you can help improve your employees' productivity and attitudes when you try appropriate, innovative techniques and use them with your own personal style of leadership, business sense, and people skills.

What Is "Performance"?

We're using the term *performance* a lot in this chapter. But what does it mean? Improving performance may be an important goal for all managers, but it will mean different things if you're manufacturing widgets, selling gizmos, or designing promotional materials for whatchamacallits. Even in the medical field, a pay-for-performance model (rewarding employees monetarily for successful results) is being adopted for physicians in some groups, and electronic record keeping is assisting managers in tracking measurable performance metrics. Among lean budgets or in fields where results matter (and realistically, where *don't* they matter?), performance becomes a hot topic.

SMART MANAGING

KNOW YOUR CONTEXT

The effective manager knows that everything is contextual. In other words, you can't expect any technique to work in every context. Before you try any technique, study your current relationship with your employees and get to know them better. Only then will you be ready to choose one of the techniques described in this chapter that might be appropriate to your situation and adapt it to your needs and your style of management.

The meaning of performance depends on your context and your particular situation. That just makes sense. It's so obvious, in fact, that you may neglect to be specific about performance with your employees.

Don't assume that your employees know what you mean by "performance." It's your responsibility to clearly define performance standards for them. Here's what each of your employees needs to know first and foremost:

- What's expected of me?
- What is my role as a part of the group and the organization?
- What's considered unacceptable performance?
- What do I have to do to reach your standards of performance?

You can set performance expectations when hiring an employee, during his or her performance review, during strategic planning, or at the start of a new project. The point is that you need to do it. You most likely know what you expect of your employees; in fact, you've probably spent hours figuring out what would be best for your department

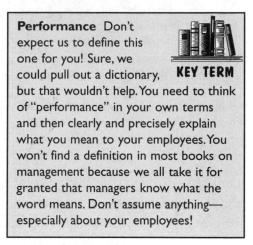

Performance Don't expect us to define this one for you! Sure, we could pull out a dictionary, **KEY TERM** but that wouldn't help. You need to think of "performance" in your own terms and then clearly and precisely explain what you mean to your employees. You won't find a definition in most books on management because we all take it for granted that managers know what the word means. Don't assume anything—especially about your employees!

and the organization. It's certainly worth a little more time and effort to make sure they understand "performance" as you understand it.

Eight Steps to Help Employees Achieve Higher Performance

The following eight steps will help you and your employees interact in ways that make you work more efficiently and effectively. These steps will help you help your employees feel more motivated on the job and build the connection between their own interests and the interests of the organization.

Step 1. Help Your Employees Stretch

Take your employees above and beyond the status quo of just doing the same job in the same way. Make their work challenging, and help them see the big picture—and their part in it!

Most people want to be better and more capable. But they may resist if they feel that higher expectations are being *imposed* on them. Make sure your employees know that you're simply trying to help them stretch and grow. You can do this by helping them set individual performance

EXCEEDING EXPECTATIONS

CAUTION

If you're bothered because some of your employees just try to meet expectations, but not exceed them, figure out why. Maybe they're simply trying to be more efficient. Maybe they're concerned about annoying their coworkers, by showing them up or looking like "the teacher's pet." Maybe they don't feel that anyone would care if they did a better job. Focus on their obstacles, not just your own goal.

goals that exceed the existing requirements of their jobs. Further, if you explain how their work adds value to the organization and how what they do affects the work of others, they can figure out ways to improve.

Step 2. Set Clear Standards

What are the standards of performance for a particular job? Identify them and be specific about the outcomes that characterize outstanding performance and the outcomes that indicate unacceptable performance. Many people found it humorous when a Supreme Court justice some years ago admitted that he couldn't define pornography, but claimed to be able to recognize it. How could he control something that he couldn't define? But that's the challenge you face as a manager: to improve performance, you've got to be able to define it.

Again, invite discussion on this matter and listen carefully to what the employee has to say. Encourage each employee to establish his or her own parameters for measuring performance based on what he or she considers to be realistic.

When you involve employees in setting performance standards, you're not just being nice; you're also being smart. Why? Three reasons:

1. Employees who are involved in developing performance standards are more likely to discuss the obstacles that might impede their efforts, so you can deal with those obstacles before they get in the way.

2. Employees who are involved in developing performance standards are more likely to understand the standards and the reasons behind them, so you won't need to work so hard to communicate them.

3. Employees who are involved in developing performance standards are more likely to accept those standards and be willing to try to meet them.

Step 3. Define the Scope of Responsibility for Employees

Make sure everyone understands who is responsible for each job activity. When employees know their roles in relationship to those of others, this reduces confusion and gives them a better sense of how they might work with their fellow employees to meet their individual objectives.

After specifying responsibilities for normal operations, consider the most probable abnormal situations and outline any shifts in responsibilities that might be necessary. If, for example, you expect someone to back up someone else when there's a large increase in orders to fill, plan for that situation and discuss specifics with employees—when, who, how. If you want some employ-

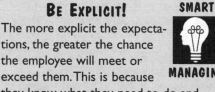

BE EXPLICIT! SMART

The more explicit the expectations, the greater the chance the employee will meet or exceed them. This is because MANAGING they know what they need to do and how they fit in. This assumes, of course, that managers will provide the tools, information, and support needed to better ensure that their employees will succeed. This may seem simple, but how many managers seem to rely on unstated assumptions or mental telepathy?

ees to put their jobs on hold and help out in receiving when several shipments show up at once, prepare contingency plans. Of course, you won't be able to prepare for everything that could affect your normal operations. But

by defining certain shifts in responsibilities ahead of time, you can help your employees understand how to best react to unexpected situations.

One of the things that can undermine employee motivation is not knowing what might be expected of them. If they know what they should do in various situations, they'll be more likely to figure out how to

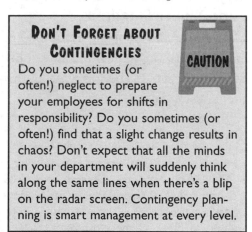

DON'T FORGET ABOUT CONTINGENCIES CAUTION

Do you sometimes (or often!) neglect to prepare your employees for shifts in responsibility? Do you sometimes (or often!) find that a slight change results in chaos? Don't expect that all the minds in your department will suddenly think along the same lines when there's a blip on the radar screen. Contingency planning is smart management at every level.

react in other situations. They'll understand that adapting to situations is part of their jobs—and that greater responsibility should increase their motivation.

Cross-functional training
This refers to training employees to know how to do most or all of the tasks their group is responsible for. Cross-functional training can help you maintain your employees' performance levels despite occasional variations in work flow or unexpected absences. Plus, you'll find that employees appreciate each other more when they've walked in each other's shoes. This helps build the feeling of community, which tends to increase employee motivation.

Once you've defined the scope of responsibilities for each employee, you may decide at some point to take the next step and broaden an employee's scope of responsibility. This can occur as the need arises, but you can also use this approach to recognize someone for taking initiative or improving his or her skills by providing *cross-functional training*. You might encourage the employee to take on a coaching or supervisory role, or suggest that he or she assume greater decision-making authority on a certain project.

The goal here is not to give employees more work. They need to know that you appreciate their efforts and want to give them the opportunity to learn more and excel on the job. If that's not the attitude you take, employees will not feel much like doing anything extra—because they won't think it's in their best interests to do so.

Step 4. Help Your Employees Buy into Higher Performance Standards

Most employees want to have a role in raising their own performance expectations. The more input an employee can provide about the job he or she is expected to perform, the more likely the employee is to buy into the new standards.

Buy in Every manager uses this term, but not in the same way. If you think that getting your employees to buy into a program means somehow compelling them to accept it, you're likely to run into problems. Employees truly buy in when they decide to invest their abilities and energies, as if they were businesspeople making a financial investment in a joint venture. So treat your employees as partners. If you do, they'll be more motivated to buy into what you're doing and to perform better.

Get your employees' perspectives on what might be involved in trying to achieve the goals you've established together. Give all your employees time to respond to what you're suggesting. Let them think it over. Invite suggestions and ideas on how to improve their performance.

When you include your employees in the improvement process, they'll share valuable information on how to meet higher standards of performance—information you might have overlooked or failed to consider.

Step 5. Document What You and Your Employees Agree On

Develop a written list of performance standards for meeting and for exceeding the expectations you've agreed on with your employees. Remember: you want your employees to continue to stretch, yet you must be sure they can attain those goals.

Be specific about what it's going to take to reach the standards in each area of job activities. Then, document those expectations. Give a copy of this document to each employee and keep one for yourself.

At employee performance reviews or on completion of projects, this document will serve as the basis for you and each of your employees to discuss and measure what was accomplished.

Step 6. Decide on a Course of Action

Once you've set standards, review the specific tasks of each person's job. Identify and discuss the areas in which each employee is skilled and qualified. Plan a course of delegation based on each employee's experience and competence.

Then—and this is important—let each employee know that once he or she has started the project and gained more insight into the intricacies

---

KNOW WHAT COUNTS

SMART
MANAGING

"What gets measured is what gets done." That's a truism that should make every manager think—a lot. Too often when we set goals and standards, we focus on what can be quantified, because there's something solid about numbers. But that focus can make you neglect some things that are important for the work environment and for the bottom line. What really matters in your department and in the rest of the organization? That's what you should measure. Remember: every manager knows how to count, but smart managers know what counts.

SMART MANAGING

Involve Your Employees

When managers meet to plan for a project, they generally work together to set goals, formulate objectives, define areas of responsibility, determine strategies, set up meetings to assess their progress, and so forth. Managers usually agree that this procedure just makes sense. It makes sense to do this with employees as well. When they're involved in the planning, they feel a sense of ownership in the project. That entrepreneurial attitude drives them to work harder and smarter to make it succeed.

of the job, you're willing to revise these expectations as necessary. You'll still keep the goals challenging, but you'll make sure they're also realistic. By doing this, you provide a safe environment so that each employee can be open and honest with you about successes and struggles along the way. In other words, you're sending out a big message that says, "It's OK to be human!"

This safe environment is good for you as well. Why? Because you too can be human. You don't have to be the traditional, superhuman manager who plans perfectly, who never changes course—who feels like a failure for acknowledging any need to change.

Step 7. Observe and Follow Up

Take time to observe how things are going along the way. Don't wait until the end of the project to check in with your employees. Depending on each person's expertise and the complexity of the task being performed, follow up and observe the job being performed while it's in progress.

SMART MANAGING

Get Out and About!

Don't wait in your office for your employees to seek you out. And don't try to wander around casually checking up on them. Go out to each employee and just start talking about the work. Find out how they're doing and what they need from you to solve problems or do something better. The point should not be just to check up, but mainly to provide the help employees need to do well.

You might want to check in more often with less experienced workers, who will need guidance and assistance, and less often with those who are more familiar with their work responsibilities, who may need nothing more from you than the assurance that you trust their judgment but are there if they need help. Following up is an important way you give employees the feedback they need about their performance and show that your job is to help them succeed.

Step 8. Be Clear About Rewards

Let employees know what to expect if they meet or exceed the standards you've developed. Be clear up front about potential rewards. Let employees know what's in it for them. And plan for them to succeed. Sure, it may be less expensive for the organization if employees fall slightly short of your expectations, because you can save on rewards. But the smart manager knows that success—even if it entails certain expenses at first—breeds success.

Then, when employees meet a standard, reward them immediately. (That's part of your plan!) You might be able to stall a creditor with a promise to pay a little later, but don't try that with your employees. The reason you need to deliver immediately is this helps employees connect the reward with the behavior.

How, specifically, might you reward and recognize employees? Well, there's always money. It's simple. But it can cost a lot, and it's impersonal. So consider also the following forms of positive reinforcement:

> **KEEP YOUR PROMISES**
> Never make a promise without a plan to deliver. If you don't have money set aside for bonuses, for example, what message does that send to the employees who earn them? That you can't be trusted? That you didn't have faith in them? On the other hand, don't make the promise of rewards the main reason for employees to perform. What you want is for employees to know that rewards are recognition of work well done and not the goal of doing the work in the first place.

- **Greater autonomy.** This tells employees you trust them to make decisions that affect their work.
- **More responsibility.** Like autonomy, this tells employees you trust and respect them and want to give them the chance to grow on the job.
- **A promotion.** This entails the former two points and also usually includes a salary increase.
- **Increased visibility within the organization.** This might involve send-

ing a memo to others, publicly recognizing the good work of an employee. It might also involve a member of top management praising the work of an individual. This type of recognition reinforces good work and says we appreciate what you're doing for us.

■ **Additional resources.** Purchase a new computer system or software, hire an assistant, and provide funds for books and seminars.

■ **Special recognition.** Award certificates of appreciation, gift certificates, or recognition from the team.

■ **A more flexible work schedule.**

■ **An opportunity to showcase their success.** Encourage speaking at a conference or presenting a case study to a management team within the organization.

■ **Material rewards.** Provide trips, dinners, and lunches.

These are just suggestions, of course, and we offer them with three important caveats:

1. **Think about the people behind the performance.** The reward should fit the achievement but also the employee(s). If you want to reward your sales team, for example, your telemarketers might appreciate a weekend trip with meals and hotel accommodations. But that prize might not excite your road warriors, the reps who live in restaurants and motels.

2. **Be fair, but be sensitive.** You probably already try to treat your employees fairly while allowing for their differences. The same guideline applies to forms of recognition. Offer choices. If you think that every employee will be pleased to receive a bottle of champagne or the chance to make a presentation, you're showing ignorance and insensitivity: many people don't drink alcohol, and many people hate speaking in public.

3. **Don't make the payoff a costly investment.** If you offer as a reward more responsibility or increased visibility within the organization, be sure you aren't courting danger by giving more responsibility to someone who can't handle stress, or increased visibility to someone who's likely to cause problems outside the department.

As noted above, don't forget to publicize achievements and their resulting rewards throughout your area and, if possible, the rest of the organization. The folks who produce your organization's newsletter are probably eager to help spread good news. (And it certainly looks good for you because it shows that you know how to motivate your employees—and how to appreciate their efforts and achievements.)

> **REWARDS AND MOTIVATION** **SMART**
> Monetary and other rewards help to reinforce performance, but as we've stressed before, don't make them the primary **MANAGING** method of influencing employee motivation. They simply don't work. Use rewards to say thanks for a job well done.

Be Realistic with Your Performance Goals

We've all experienced the pressure from someone who expects more of us than we can deliver. Does it motivate us? Surely not. In fact, it can do the opposite, slipping us into a pit of despair and depression.

To motivate employees with your goals, make sure they're achievable. Mac Anderson, author and founder of the successful corporate motivational companies, Successories and Simple Truths, states that you should also include short-term, achievable goals along with any larger objectives. This way, you can give your employees confidence in their abilities, and celebrate each milestone along the way. Your ultimate goal will gradually grow closer as a result.

Expect the Best—and Don't Let It Surprise You

If you have high expectations for your employees, you possess a powerful and effective tool for improving performance within your organization. It's actually pretty natural, and almost unavoidable, for us to form expectations of others. Research has found that in an organization, our expectations of others can be tied directly to productivity, profitability, and

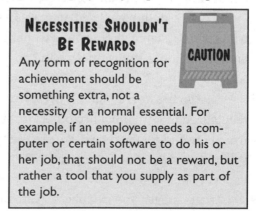

> **NECESSITIES SHOULDN'T BE REWARDS** **CAUTION**
> Any form of recognition for achievement should be something extra, not a necessity or a normal essential. For example, if an employee needs a computer or certain software to do his or her job, that should not be a reward, but rather a tool that you supply as part of the job.

the organization's overall success.

Think back to Chapter 2 and our discussion of Douglas McGregor and his concept of Theory X and Theory Y managers. Both types of managers influence the performance of their employees, but in different ways. Managers are likely to get what they expect from their employees—but that may not always be good.

There's an old story about a boy who did poorly in school from the start. When he suddenly started doing much better in fifth grade, his former teachers were amazed. Curious about the transformation, they went to talk with his teacher, who was new to the school.

"We're all surprised at the success you've had with Bobby," the former teachers said. "Why is he learning so much better now? How are you getting such good work out of such a stupid boy?"

"Well," the teacher answered, "I just don't treat him like he's stupid."

Performance is often a question of expectations. Teachers form expectations, which then influence how they interact with their students. Managers form expectations, which then influence, in a similar way, how they interact with their employees. When you don't expect much, employees sense that, and it affects their desire to do well. The point is that people naturally try to live up to our expectations—or down to them. So, how does a smart manager set his or her expectations?

Expect Better Performance

Expectations influence behavior. To put it simply, you, as a manager, will get better performance from your people if you expect it of them. This behavioral phenomenon is often referred to as the Pygmalion Effect.

In Greek mythology, Pygmalion was a sculptor and the King of Cyprus who carved a statue of a beautiful woman. He fell in love with his creation and, in response to his prayers, the goddess Venus endowed the statue with life.

The Greeks developed this myth from the reality around them. They recognized that we influence others through our expectations. It's just as true thousands of years later. We use the term *Pygmalion Effect* to refer to this phenomenon of finding in objects, situations, or people what we expect to find in them.

As a manager, you can play a Pygmalion-like role in developing your employees. Your expectations can lead them to perform better—and to sometimes even surpass your expectations.

Science Supports the Pygmalion Effect

> **Pygmalion Effect** Put simply, people naturally tend to try to meet your expectations of them. Of course, **KEY TERM** you need to communicate your expectations; you can't expect divine intervention, as when Venus helped Pygmalion!

The Pygmalion Effect is not just a myth. The theory has been tested over time in carefully validated scientific studies. Consider the following study results:

- Test scores of children rise when the children are told that they're expected to do well.
- The performance of workers improves when their managers are told beforehand that they're going to be leading a group of exceptionally bright and high-potential employees, because the managers tend to treat those workers as being capable of superior performance.
- Workers achieve higher levels of performance when their supervisors tell them up front what performance is expected of them.

These studies and others underscore the validity of the Pygmalion Effect: you can significantly influence the feelings, attitudes, and behaviors of those around you if you communicate your expectations, explicitly and implicitly.

Take a moment to think about the people around you: your employees, your fellow managers, close friends, neighbors, children. Isn't it true that the way we see all of the people in our lives affects how we treat them? And isn't it also true that the way we treat them often affects how they behave toward us?

Taking Advantage of the Pygmalion Effect to Improve Employee Performance

To use the Pygmalion Effect to improve employee performance and motivation, you have to show you're committed to your people by taking the following three steps:

1. Create a high-performance environment.
2. Share the rewards of successful performance.

> **SMART**
>
>
>
> **MANAGING**
>
> ## Pygmalion in Management
>
> Consider this comment by J. Sterling Livingston, author of "Pygmalion in Management," a 1969 article published in the *Harvard Business Review*: "If he [the manager] has confidence in his ability to develop and stimulate them [employees] to high levels of performance, he will expect much of them and will treat them with the confidence that his expectations will be met. But if he has doubts about his ability to stimulate them, he will expect less of them and will treat them with less confidence." In other words, the manager's expectations will affect the performance of his employees—for better or for worse. It's not a bad quote maybe to hang on your office wall.

3. Inspire others to higher-level performance.

Step 1. Create a High-Performance Environment

To tap and develop the motivation within your employees, you must deliberately create an environment conducive to higher levels of performance. In this environment, you and your people are focused and clear about your objectives, the work is stimulating and challenging, people feel appreciated and respected, you and your people have the resources you need, and people help and support one another without being asked.

Before you can create a higher-performance environment, you'll have to assess your current environment. Only then can you determine what you'll need to do to go from where you are to where you want to be.

> **CAUTION**
>
> ## Trust and Meeting Expectations
>
> Beware! Your success in using the Pygmalion Effect to improve employee performance and motivation depends on a relationship of commitment and trust. If you have only expectations, without a supportive relationship with your employees, you may see people work down to the level of commitment you show and the level of trust you inspire.

Involve your employees in this assessment. That's a necessity, to show your commitment to them and to inspire their trust in you from the start. Solicit their input and opinions. For starters, here are some questions you might ask your employees:

- What is challenging about your work?

- From what sources do you get a sense of job satisfaction?
- Do you feel appreciated?
- Do you get the recognition you deserve?
- What has motivated you to work harder in the past?
- Whom do you count on in a crunch?
- Where do you get your support?
- What are your greatest obstacles to getting your work done?
- What resources do you need that you don't currently have?

After you've collected this information from employees, do something useful with it! Nothing instills cynicism in employees more than participating in a survey and then seeing no improvements result from it. It's important then to use the information you gather to improve your organization's environment in order to encourage and build employee motivation to perform.

Do all you can to show your employees that your actions are meaningful and sincere. Consider the following strategies:

- Share the data you've collected about the current work environment, ask for everyone's ideas and suggestions for improvement, publish a plan, and let your people put it into action.
- Continue to emphasize your own personal commitment to the department and your team. Praise the commitment of your staff.
- Connect the success of the team to the success of the organization.

In other words, use strategies like these to ensure that management values employees and wants to take actions to benefit both employees and the organization.

Step 2. Share the Rewards of Successful Performance

An important goal of any motivation program is to help employees feel that the work itself is a reward. It's like students in school; those who perform best are really interested in the subject and like learning for its own sake, not just to get a good grade. But you reinforce that natural motivation when you arrange for your employees to enjoy other rewards that result from their work.

If you want to help your employees maintain a high level of motivation on the job, you can share the rewards with all those who have contributed to the organization's success. This idea is not commonly understood or implemented.

In many organizations, pay levels have more to do with seniority than with performance. Employees doing the same work may receive substantially different pay, based on length of employment. Certainly there is merit in paying those with more seniority more money if their experience allows them to add more value to the organization than a less experienced employee.

However, in today's workplace, where most jobs are interdependent, you want to improve every employee's motivation, so it's a good idea to share success in some equitable manner with all who have contributed. In doing this, you're providing employees tangible proof that they're really making a difference by what they do, not just by how long they've been doing it.

Here are some methods you might consider for doing this:

- **Special rewards.** When an employee or group of employees improves a process or a product or saves the organization money, share part of those benefits with the employee or group. This shows that you recognize that special contribution and are encouraging them to continue making such contributions. The plan may include a percentage of the financial benefit to the organization from the employee's efforts or it may be a specific amount.

- **Profit-sharing and bonuses.** One important reason your employees are there is to help the company make a profit and grow. It makes sense then to share the gains with employees. Though many companies try to evaluate the contribution of different employees to the company's success, such efforts are usually based on false assumptions. Since the success of any employee depends on other employees doing their jobs as well, it makes more sense to share profits and create a bonus pool that recognizes this. A good way is to set up a plan that gives employees the equivalent of an equal number of weeks' pay as a bonus for their efforts during the year. Though employees receive different amounts because of different salary levels, they all share equitably in the organization's profits. This tells all employees that the organization appreciates their efforts.

Besides pay, there are other ways you can help employees share in the rewards of successful performance. Here are some ways you might do that:

- **Recognition and praise.** You may be amazed at the response of employees to simple compliments for work well done. In your compliments, you should be specific about what the employee did and how it helped the organization. It's best to give face-to-face compliments to the employee and then follow up by sending him or her a memo of appreciation—which you copy for the employee's file.

- **Training, seminars, and workshops.** Giving employees these special learning opportunities, both within and outside the organization, encourages personal and professional development—and often increases motivation as well. It tells employees that you value their performance and want to give them more opportunities. Don't forget, in doing this, to give employees immediate opportunities to use their new skills so the training pays off and they take it seriously.

- **Inexpensive morale boosters.** When a team does a good job on some project, perhaps a small process improvement plan or working together to solve a problem that's come up, you can boost morale by ordering pizzas or submarine sandwiches for lunch parties or maybe inviting employees to your home for a barbecue. Below are 14 ways in which you can recognize employee performance and contributions to the organization's success:

1. A day off with pay
2. Plaques
3. Travel awards
4. A letter of praise
5. Dinner at the boss's house
6. A free family photo session
7. Lunch on the organization
8. Dinner on the organization
9. Specialty items, such as T-shirts, pens, and tote bags featuring the organization's logo
10. An extra break
11. A two-hour lunch

12. A three-day weekend

13. A massage or manicure

14. A magazine subscription

Step 3. Inspire Others to Higher-Level Performance

Great leaders are often inspirational. They foster optimism. As a manager, you can create an environment that helps people climb to the next level of achievement, satisfaction, and excellence.

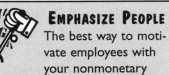 **EMPHASIZE PEOPLE**
The best way to motivate employees with your nonmonetary rewards is to emphasize people. When you recognize employees with praise, ceremonies, or perks, do so in ways that involve their peers. People rarely succeed alone—and they rarely want to celebrate their achievements that way.

Creating a work environment where people really love what they do and feel motivated to do great work takes certain skills. But if you develop these skills, you'll develop an energized and creative work team.

Here are 12 techniques to help you inspire others to higher-level performance:

1. Walk the talk. Be the role model for what you expect in others.

2. Convey enthusiasm in what you do.

3. Remind others that problems can be overcome.

4. Recognize attempts to improve effectiveness and productivity— even when they don't necessarily work.

5. Recognize people who overcome obstacles to achieve results.

6. Keep an open mind and focus on the positive side of new ideas.

7. Encourage people to talk with you about their feelings.

8. Meet with people—individually or in groups—when morale is low. Express optimism and faith in the team. Expect the best from people. Expect that they will excel.

9. Make work fun.

10. See the humor in your own mistakes. Laugh more.

11. Focus on small, but significant wins, not just the big deals.

12. Celebrate a lot.

Performance: Drive and Direction

In the first three chapters of this book, we focused on the *drive*—how managers can understand and influence the forces that compel us to do things. In this chapter, we shifted our focus to *direction*—how managers must specify expectations and set standards to turn motivation into performance.

It's a question of balance. As a manager, you must try to align the individual needs and interests of your employees with the mission and goals of the organization. Since you're reading this book, we can assume you realize that the purpose of your position is not just to pursue that mission and achieve that goal as if you were in control of a set of robots. If that's all that matters, then your people won't stay with you. But you also know that employees need more than motivation, more than a feeling of satisfaction. If that's all you've got, your organization may not last very long.

So, in this chapter I've tried to bring together *drive* and *direction*, focusing on how you can link motivation to performance. That focus should guide you as you read the remaining chapters.

Manager's Checklist for Chapter 4

☑ You improve performance by working with what motivates your employees to do their best and eliminating obstacles that keep your employees from experiencing higher levels of job satisfaction.

☑ Be specific with your employees about what's meant by "performance." They need to know what's expected of them, what's considered unacceptable, and what it might take for them to reach the standards of performance that you and your employees set together.

☑ Your expectations affect the behavior of your employees. If you expect better performance and trust employees to deliver, you're likely to get it. This behavioral phenomenon is known as the Pygmalion Effect.

☑ Create an environment that encourages and supports higher levels of performance. Be specific in setting your objectives, try to stimulate and challenge your employees, provide the resources they need, and show how much you appreciate and respect them.

☑ Check out SimpleTruths.com for affordable books and videos that build teams and motivate employees to greater success and fulfillment.

☑ Share the rewards of success—but remember that the best motivation is intrinsic.

☑ Employees who find satisfaction in doing their jobs will usually try to perform better.

Chapter 5

Helping Employees Accept Responsibility for Motivation

Show People How to Step up to the Plate, Be Accountable, and Drive Results

Helping employees attend to their own motivational needs is one of the most powerful interventions you can make to increase your organization's potential for success. When employees rely on themselves to stay motivated, rather than on others, they're accepting self-responsibility. And when they accept responsibility for themselves, they understand that they also have responsibility for their success.

As a manager, you're used to taking responsibility for yourself and for others. That's what managing is all about, right? Not necessarily. That ability (urge?) to assume total responsibility may be a key reason why you've been successful and how you've gotten to where you are now, but it's not necessarily the best way to manage—or to positively influence your employees' motivation.

It may be time for you to aim a little higher and reduce your responsibility. Your goal is to create a truly self-motivating organization—one that inspires employees to take responsibility for their own motivation.

Motivating People with Responsibility and Authority

Managers often think in terms of giving their employees motivation. But that's not what you should give your employees if you want them to be motivated. Instead, broadly speaking, you need to give them

- The responsibility for achieving something
- The authority to do it their own way

This *empowerment* unleashes tremendous energy and motivation. When you give your employees responsibility and authority together, they feel that you trust them and value them. They won't want to disappoint themselves by not using this authority properly to do work. You've said, in so many words, "I trust you and know that you're going to make sound decisions in your own best interests and in the interests of everyone."

KEY TERM — **Empower** The dictionary defines this term as "to give power or authority to someone." It might be better to think about it as acknowledging and releasing the power within each employee to do his or her best work. Empowered employees have the authority and responsibility to do what's necessary to get their jobs done efficiently and effectively.

Smart managers recognize this as a win-win situation. Your employees win because they're empowered and motivated. You win because you get better performance and happier employees without having to put forth the effort to entice them from the outside.

It makes good sense to transfer the responsibility for staying motivated to individual employees—because that's where it lies in the first place. And you can do it in steps, by delegating important tasks. Just be sure to give your employees the responsibility and authority necessary to make important decisions and act on them. And make sure they understand that you're giving them the full responsibility and the full authority. Let them know you understand that things might not always work right, but that you and your employees are always learning from your experiences—which are always opportunities to improve. Being empowered while having to worry that you might make a mistake is no empowerment at all. Then let them get to the task!

Let People Be Powerful and Magnify Their Potential

Even before empowerment became a management buzzword, smart managers were already familiar with the basic principle: when workers feel strong, confident, and capable, they can accomplish more—and usually do. Those same managers also knew that when workers feel unappreciated or insignificant to the overall operation, and when they lack responsibility and authority, they tend to perform down to low management expectations. They also tend to complain. Managers can magnify their employees' potential, or they can shrink people and make them feel small and insignificant. Neither is an accident. It's a choice, either way.

That's why smart managers have believed in empowerment, even if they might not have called it by that name. Empowerment challenges managers to do something quite unconventional: give their power away. Many managers resist this notion. They like being in power. Throughout history, people have noticed the extent to which power can attract and intoxicate. On the other hand, power can also enslave and corrupt.

Think about it for a moment. What is your job? Why are you necessary to your organization? You're not there to hold power. That's just a resource, a means toward an end. Your responsibility is to use your authority to get results, to help your employees perform better. So if you can improve performance by sharing your power, that's what you ought to do.

By giving away your power, you allow your employees to share your responsibility and authority. They find greater motivation in their work—and you progressively liberate yourself from the burden of using whips, carrots, or other external forces to try to influence them.

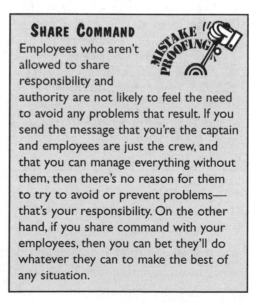

SHARE COMMAND
Employees who aren't allowed to share responsibility and authority are not likely to feel the need to avoid any problems that result. If you send the message that you're the captain and employees are just the crew, and that you can manage everything without them, then there's no reason for them to try to avoid or prevent problems— that's your responsibility. On the other hand, if you share command with your employees, then you can bet they'll do whatever they can to make the best of any situation.

This doesn't mean you still don't have responsibility for the performance of your employees in the eyes of management. It just means that you've given employees more responsibility to execute their tasks without someone looking over their shoulder. It means you've given them the tools, information, and training they need to do their work. And it means that your employees look to you to remove obstacles and support them in their work. It means, in other words, that you're taking actions to improve performance by making your employees responsible for that performance.

Remember the importance of encouraging entrepreneurial thinking that I discussed in Chapter 3? Giving away your power is another way to do that. Empowerment makes people feel and act like entrepreneurs—like business owners who have a stake in it all. Thus, it increases your employees' motivation to do a good job.

Not a Housekeeper, But an Entrepreneur

Mary—a housekeeper I met at the Four Seasons Hotel in Austin, Texas, while on a business trip—clearly sees herself as a one-woman business enterprise. She exudes this vision in her attitude and in her determination to "own her own floor." Mary makes it clear that she doesn't see herself as a hotel housekeeper. Instead, she embraces a total "entrepreneurial attitude" about her work.

SMART MANAGING

GIVE POWER AWAY

You become more powerful when you give your power away. Why? Because when you empower others, you build alliances with them. They recognize that it's in their best interest to work harder and smarter, to take full advantage of their abilities to perform well, because everybody benefits from the results.

"These are *my* rooms," she says. "This floor is *my* business, no one else's. I have to take good care of my customers. They know I care, and I will do what I have to do to make their stay a great one. I don't need permission to take charge and do what's right. I just do it. People think I own this floor—and I do."

Is Mary empowered? Perhaps not formally. As she puts it, "I don't need permission to take charge and do what's right. I just do it." If her managers are smart, they will let Mary take charge of "her floor," because they know her attitude benefits the hotel guests.

But what if her managers felt threatened by her entrepreneurial attitude? What if they decided Mary shouldn't feel free to take action without first getting permission? Well, they'd certainly be exercising their authority and showing her who's boss. And if that were the essence of their job description, they'd certainly be performing very well. But their job is probably to make sure that the Four Seasons provides its guests with the most enjoyable, positively memorable visit possible. Given that, then their "boss" behavior would hurt their clients and ruin the enthusiastic work spirit of one of their housekeepers. That's a high price to pay for exercising their authority and keeping Mary from "taking charge of the floor." After all, Mary takes charge not to usurp anyone's authority, but to be more able to deliver good services to customers.

Many employees don't feel this entrepreneurial spirit, especially if they don't work directly with customers—and if they've become accustomed to simply doing what they're told. They work for the money and to avoid criticism, punishment, and losing their jobs. They're motivated by need and fear. Entrepreneurial thinking? Hah! They're not expected (or even allowed) to think, and they're certainly not likely to feel as though they have a share in the organization and its success or failure.

When employees feel this way, when they don't feel motivated to do anything beyond what's required of them, you must take action. You need to drive home the message of self-power, self-importance, self-accountability, and self-responsibility. You need to help your employees understand that this is not something they get from someone else; it's something they initiate on their own.

How can you help employees accept self-responsibility and motivate themselves? It's not hard. Share your authority and responsibility with them, and you help them develop self-power. Stress the importance of their jobs within the context of the entire organization, particularly with respect to your customers, and you help employees feel important and accountable. Build an environment of trust and collaboration and you help them free themselves from factors that undermine their positive motivation. Then employees learn to rely on themselves—not on others—for their motivation.

Sharing Your Power

There are a lot of bad managers out there and a lot of employees working without much motivation. This situation is so common that it's made a millionaire out of Scott Adams, creator of the *Dilbert* cartoon empire.

We all enjoy the cartoons. But you should recognize that even if the Dilbert situation is widespread, it isn't inevitable. Don't get sucked into accepting the Dilbert mentality. Smart managers know that employees must get beyond the us versus them attitude, beyond accepting a sense of fatalism and resignation as the norm, and beyond pouring their energies into complaining and resistance. This just gets in the way of performance.

You need to make self-responsibility and empowerment the foundation for the way you manage. Go beyond the Dilbert management characters, share authority and responsibility, and allow your employees to accept responsibility for finding motivation to perform better and to develop.

That approach really pays off, as the Ritz-Carlton hotel chain has discovered. Those folks really know how to share power!

Ritz-Carlton employees are authorized—right here, right now, no questions asked—to fix any customer's problem and spend up to $2,000 to do it! That's on-the-spot authority, the power to act immediately. They don't need to page the manager or wait until the assistant manager gets back from a break. They can handle the situation themselves and better serve their guests. That means Ritz-Carlton is more competitive—and that each of its employees is more motivated to do his or her best for the guests and the hotel.

That's giving power away. Trusting every employee with the authority to invest $2,000 to solve a problem? You probably know plenty of company vice presidents who aren't authorized to spend $500 without three cosigners and a really good excuse!

Ritz-Carlton's management model is exemplary, not only for empowering its employees, but also for capitalizing on the potential for employee self-responsibility. That's just part of the company way of treating its employees with respect. It's no wonder Ritz-Carlton won the Malcolm Baldrige National Quality Award in 1992—the first hotel company to do so.

(Note: The Ritz-Carlton Hotels are now part of Marriott International, another exemplary organization that focuses on empowering employees and memorable customer service.)

The Power of Belief: Setting "Perfect Present-Tense Personalized" Goals

Pete Thomas entered NBC's *The Biggest Loser* in 2005 with no concern about winning or losing. Instead, he just wanted help losing weight. He knew that he would lose the weight somehow, and has since gone on to make millions by helping others do the same thing.

Tipping the scales at 416 pounds, Pete hadn't learned about proper nutrition or exercise due to his childhood lifestyle—frequent moves led by a mother with serious mental illness.

While he didn't win the grand prize, he did lose the weight. So much of it, in fact, that when NBC called him back after he'd been voted off and announced that they would be handing out a second prize to the person who had lost the most fat after leaving the show, Thomas stepped it up and claimed the $100,000.

He credits his success with the fact that he wasn't afraid to learn what he needed to do to lose the weight. But beyond that, he had the belief that he would lose the weight. He developed what he calls "perfect present-tense personalized" goals: stating the goal as if it is being achieved. Instead of focusing on the weight he had to lose, he focused on the outcome he wanted to achieve. He even created a mnemonic device for himself to reinforce this: "I feel sexy, strong, and great, as I maintain my weight at or around 238." Today, he consults on weight management, and speaks to corporations on the principles he used for his success.

Redefining the Manager-Employee Relationship

If you're ready to start giving your power away to positively influence your your employees' motivation, begin by *redefining the relationship between you and your employees*. Here are a few ways to start:

- Enlarge your employees' circle of influence. Increase the ways in which they interact with other employees, so they play a greater role in the operation, to develop their sense of belonging and ownership.

- Increase signature authority for your employees.
- Make sure that employees don't feel restricted by their titles or positions.
- Define jobs more broadly, leaving room for creativity and autonomy.
- Eliminate cumbersome employee rules and policies.
- Reduce unnecessary approval steps.
- Support good judgment and common sense.

SMART MANAGING

THE BEST LEADER

The ideas I've been talking about so far in this chapter aren't really so new. The Zen sage Lao Tsu wrote many centuries ago:

A leader is best
When people barely know he exists,
Not so good when people obey and acclaim him,
Worse when they despise him.
Fail to honor people,
They fail to honor you.
But of the good leader, who talks little,
When his work is done, his aim fulfilled,
They will say, "We did this work ourselves."

Think about it.

Help Employees Take Control of Their Lives

In today's business environment, managers are being required to provide more and more decision-making discretion to their employees to meet the continually changing and demanding needs of customers, shareholders, and suppliers. This requires managers to support employees in taking control of their lives.

Some managers will consider this bad news because it means they need to share their power and to trust their employees more. They may resist it, but the shift seems inevitable.

MISTAKE PROOFING

REDUCE YOUR "LAWS"

Many organizations function like most governments: they keep amassing policies and rules. Rarely do organizations actually reduce their "laws."

Nordstrom, a famous clothing retailer based in Seattle, is an exception. The company has a distinct aversion to corporate policy clutter and tons of unnecessary employee policies. As a result, there's only one rule published in Nordstrom's employee handbook:

Rule #1: Use your good judgment in all situations. There will be no additional rules.

If you're smart, you'll welcome the change. By delegating more and giving employees more discretion, you help your employees expand their minds, develop their talents and skills, and discover untapped abilities. As a result, your employees are more personally motivated. They are more committed to their work and they involve more of themselves. The result for you as their manager and for the organization as a whole: improved performance.

Choice Drives and Affirms

When we have choices, we feel a greater sense of control and self-responsibility. That's just basic human nature. When an employee is free to make choices about the particular role he or she will play in the organization, that freedom serves as motivation because choice involves commitment.

Here are a few choices employees make when they feel empowered. Would your employees feel comfortable making the following statements?

- I have the choice to be strong, not weak and powerless.
- I have the choice to adopt the mentality that I don't need "formal" authority to make a significant difference.
- I have the choice to make a difference in this organization. My efforts are directly reflected in the bottom line.
- I have the choice to behave in a way that positively affects the people I work with. I know I can set the tone and affect the attitudes of others.
- I have the choice to bring enthusiasm and energy to my job. I know that when I do this, I can positively affect my customers, both internal and external.
- I have the choice to take an interest in this organization. I want to find out how it all started and how it became what it is today.
- I have the choice to take responsibility for my actions and for what bothers me. When I come upon a difficult situation, I must approach it as "my" problem.
- I have the choice, even if I feel the situation is unfair or not right, to try to find a solution before seeking outside help.
- I have the choice to accept what I cannot change. I will look for ways to minimize the situation's effect on me and my coworkers.

■ I have the choice to acknowledge that I have chosen to work here. I am not a prisoner. I can choose to move on if I so desire without deflating the morale of others.

You might want to print out this list of choices and post copies around your workplace. You should also put a copy on your office wall to remind you of your employees' choices and to serve as a sign of your commitment to maintaining a climate of choice.

SMART MANAGING

SUSTAINING MOTIVATION

To sustain your own motivation, you must identify and understand your motives and then take committed action on them. To sustain the motivations of others, you must identify and understand their motives and then encourage them to take committed action on those motives. That's the essence of helping your employees assume and maintain responsibility for their own motivation.

Warning: Such notions as these are inspirational—but don't put up signs like these on your walls unless you really mean it. Employees will take them with a grain of salt, and it can undermine your efforts to help them become more motivated.

Helping Employees Take Responsibility for Their Own Motivation

Encourage employees to believe in themselves. When you catch employees "putting themselves down," help them to understand the impact of negative self-talk. For example, you might hear an employee say, "I can't do this, and I don't want to try anymore." You need to remind this person that most things are hard when you first try, but with some help from others, and practice, the hard stuff gets easier. Explain how we tend to act down or up to our self-image. Help your employees to see the positive sides of themselves and to work on building a strong and healthy sense of self-esteem.

You might even have your employees draw up contracts with themselves. (Emphasize that it's completely voluntary, something they do on their own, for themselves. You won't even read it.) Ask each of them to explain in writing why he or she has the ability and talent to succeed. Have

AN AGREEMENT FOR YOU

TRICKS OF THE TRADE

When you conduct the contract exercise in positive thinking, you want to discourage employees from focusing on obstacles that keep them from improving. But if you notice that any of them mention things in the workplace that negatively impact their attitudes or performance, take the opportunity to improve your performance as a manager.

Draw up and sign your own agreement in which you commit to reducing or eliminating the obstacles that keep your employees from realizing their potential. It's a good way to support their efforts and inspire them to improve. Then post this agreement where you'll be able to read it regularly.

them detail and commit to what they will do to strive toward excellence. And encourage them to describe just how they will execute this agreement.

Have each employee date and sign his or her contract, put it in an envelope addressed to himself or herself, and seal it. Tell employees that you'll mail their contracts back to them in 90 days. This can be a powerful strategy because when people know they'll be reminded of their accountability they tend to take their commitments more seriously. Remind them that you won't even look at their contracts because it's not an agreement with you, but with themselves.

Help employees develop goals for self-motivation. Goals help us look forward because they focus our energies and allow us to measure our progress. It's important for you, as a manager, to help your employees set meaningful goals. When you help them, make sure each of the goals is SMART:

S – pecific   What exactly do they intend to achieve?
M – easurable   How will they determine if they've achieved the goal?
A – chievable   Is this something they can do?
R – ealistic   Is this possible within the situation?
T – ime-based   When will they achieve the goal?

The Bridge People Need to Achieve Their Goals

The ability to stay self-motivated and accept responsibility is the bridge between setting goals and reaching them. It's essential for success, no matter what the endeavor. It's always the driving force behind our achievements.

How do you help your employees build and use this bridge? Try some or all of the following strategies:

Help employees face fear. Fear prevents us from fulfilling our innermost desires. It causes stress, anxiety, and panic, often undermining the plans we've made for ourselves and impeding our efforts to attain our goals.

To help employees overcome their fears, encourage them to recognize and talk openly about what scares them most, and to then take action in spite of their fears. When employees are working toward their goals, fears soon dissipate and self-confidence begins to strengthen.

Help employees focus on the end result. Have your employees visualize what success might look like. Encourage them to create a vivid and clear picture of success that will make them want to drive toward it and be a part of it. To assist in the visualization process, you might suggest that employees draw a color picture to represent the desirable result they seek. (This should be voluntary, of course.) Some may want to display their drawings where others can easily see them, while others may want to keep theirs in a drawer. If visualization is going to work, it's got to be *their* picture, *their* way.

> **TRICKS OF THE TRADE**
>
> **CAUSES OF FEAR**
>
> It's often difficult for people to express their fears. You'll be better able to help your employees if you understand what's most likely causing their fears.
>
> Here's what people tend to fear most:
>
> - That they won't belong, that they'll be rejected.
> - That they'll be seen as vulnerable and weak.
> - That they might not measure up
> - That they'll appear inferior.

Help employees identify and satisfy their emotional needs. We're all driven by our emotional needs as well as our career goals. If you better understand a few of the basic emotional needs of your employees, it will be easier for you to support your people in fulfilling their needs.

Although a list of emotional needs can go on forever and vary greatly according to the individual, here are a few that show up frequently in the workplace:

- **Recognition and praise.** It's essential to have others acknowledge our work. Without recognition and praise, we feel as though our efforts are unnoticed or unappreciated.

- **Achievement and advancement.** Achievement gives us purpose. It reinforces our confidence because we've demonstrated our competence. Advancement is a measure of our success and makes us feel as though our lives are expanding in a positive direction.
- **Belonging.** Being part of a team or a family provides us with comfort and a sense of security. Belonging enriches our lives.
- **Challenge and excitement.** To grow mentally, emotionally, personally, and professionally, we need to be challenged. We also need a sense of "newness" in our lives. Excitement stimulates our senses. The alternative is to shrink and stagnate, to become bored and dissatisfied.
- **Pride and confidence.** We need to be proud of our work and of what we do, and we must be confident in our abilities and our worth. That's why some workers can find great joy and happiness in their jobs, no matter how routine they may seem.
- **Friends and family.** Personal relationships provide us with the important network of support we all need, both on the job and at home.

Encourage Accountability

Being accountable means taking responsibility for your actions and their outcomes. You can probably count on most of your employees to do what you ask them to do. But that's not accountability. (In fact, when employees are reacting to instructions, orders, or recommendations from a manager, they often tend to hold the manager responsible for the outcomes.)

Accountability goes beyond the performance of a task.

> **SEEING THE BIG PICTURE**
>
> What's the best way to encourage accountability among your employees? By helping them understand and appreciate the role they play in the big organizational picture. There's a saying that should make every manager think: "No individual raindrop ever considers itself responsible for the flood." And more positively: "No individual raindrop ever can take credit for the flowers."

When employees have a sense of accountability, they feel responsible for their work and the results they achieve.

Tips for Holding Employees Accountable

How do you convey accountability? How do you encourage your employees to feel responsible for their work and the results they achieve? Here are a few suggestions:

- **Get a commitment to performance requirements.** Work with each of your employees to develop a list of mutually acceptable performance criteria. Then, put these expectations in writing. By doing this, you establish a basis for setting accountability requirements with the employee.

- **Conduct performance reviews.** Base performance reviews on the expectations you've put in writing beforehand. When employees understand that you're connecting expectations and reviews, they'll develop a greater sense of accountability. Typically, what gets measured gets done.

- **Establish rewards and penalties.** When employees accomplish what they set out to do, recognize their achievements. When employees establish a pattern of disregarding the seriousness of their commitments and objectives, appropriate penalties may be necessary.

- **Demonstrate a low tolerance for mediocrity.** Let your leadership style show your values and beliefs. Serve as a model for excellence. Show employees by the way you work that excellence is the only option. By taking this perspective with your own work, you show that mediocrity is not acceptable.

SMART

MANAGING

IT'S WITHIN YOU AND WITHIN THEM

Whatever actions you take as a manager, your ultimate goal should be to help each of your employees feel motivated from within. Help employees accept a sense of accountability that will guide and inspire them, even if they're working alone.

When Ffyona Campbell set out to walk those 16,088 kilometers across Africa, from Cape Town to Tangiers, it amazed everyone. When asked why she was doing what she was doing, she replied, "Because I said I would." When asked who she said this to, she answered, "Myself."

Why Do Any of Us Do What We Do?

Starting April 2, 1991, Ffyona Campbell walked the length of Africa—16,088 kilometers from Cape Town to Tangiers. She walked not only through jungles and deserts, but also through a 400-mile-wide mine-field. Her extraordinary efforts earned her the title "The Greatest Walker of Them All."

Why did Campbell do this? Why do people—whether teachers, pilots, musicians, doctors, or writers—do the extraordinary on their own and without provocation? It's definitely *not* to get a raise or a big promotion.

What pushes each and every one of us to go the extra mile, to climb the highest mountains, or, in this case, to walk 10,000 miles across the most treacherous terrain in the world? Self-motivation—motivation from within each person's heart and mind.

As I said in the beginning of this chapter, there's no greater force than self-motivation. It's perhaps the only motivation worth exploring.

Manager's Checklist for Chapter 5

☑ The most powerful intervention you can make for your organization is to encourage your employees to attend to their own motivational needs. Employees who rely on themselves rather than on others to stay motivated are accepting self-responsibility.

☑ Don't try to give your employees motivation. Give them the responsibility for achieving something and the authority to do it their own way. Then they'll find their own motivation.

☑ Share your power with your employees. Begin by redefining your relationship with them: enlarge their circles of influence, increase signature authority, define their jobs more broadly, reduce rules and policies, and support good judgment and common sense at all times.

☑ Practice "Perfect Present-Tense Personalized" goal setting.

☑ Allow your employees to make more choices. This will give them a greater sense of control and self-responsibility.

☑ Hold your employees accountable for their actions and the outcomes. When employees have a sense of accountability, they feel greater motivation to perform well and they get to be part of something greater than themselves.

Riding the Waves of Hope and Trust

Managers Who Trust Themselves Will Trust Others

Motivation is partly based on a vision of hope—the hope of finding meaningful purpose and reaching greater success from our efforts—hope of a better future for ourselves, our families, friends, and coworkers. In other words, hope is like an ocean of possibilities and represents what life could be. When we are motivated to believe in the possibilities, a brighter tomorrow often surfaces. However, for this concept to gain traction in the workplace, first there has to be a strong level of trust between managers and their employees.

If you think about it, levels of trust among teams and within organizations, big and small, often come in waves—and like the organizations themselves, some waves are big, and some are just ripples. Trust is the perpetual wave of management on which all great leaders feel compelled to ride and navigate.

As Tom Peters and other management gurus have predicted over the years, more than technology or training, trust is going to be the core leadership value and soft-skill competency of the decade that all managers must learn to instill and navigate if they are to survive and thrive! So get ready to ride the undulating waves of trust when you see them coming, learn to encourage others to trust in themselves in choppy waters, and then start building trust throughout the organization as one of the most important leadership initiatives and competencies you'll ever implement. Trust is everything.

A Surfer-Leader Brands Trust at MedAmerica Billing Services, Inc.

"Trust is how we roll," says James V. Proffitt, the engaging and high-energy COO and president of MedAmerica Billing Services, Inc. (MBSI), based in Modesto, California. Proffitt is not only a beloved and trusted leader at MBSI, he's an avid surfer and skateboarder! When Proffitt talks about his extreme passion for inspiring motivation and trust in teams at MBSI, he often refers to navigating the ocean's waves on his surfboard or riding his skateboard—"It takes trust!" says Proffitt. "Trust in yourself and trust in others."

Hire the Best, Trust Your People, or Wipe Out!

According to Profitt, "MBSI hires active, intelligent, motivated, and trustworthy employees to make things happen day in and day out. Trustworthy employees blow up the box and do amazing things because they, too, are trusted by their managers and feel empowered to make decisions that change the course of the company."

He goes on to say, "It's highly motivating! It's not enough anymore to develop and train employees on the basics. We need to develop their emotional intelligence (EQ) as well, by making trust a core competency for leadership success—a competency that expands everyone's knowledge base because they feel empowered to get out there and innovate, create, be flexible, and ride the varying waves of leadership success."

Just like in surfing or skateboarding, Proffitt knows that managers can make mistakes. "If you mess up, who cares? It doesn't mean you wiped out. Get back up on your board and ride!" says Proffitt. "Trusted employees are not afraid to learn from

A SURFER-LEADER WHO FOUNDED PATAGONIA Patagonia founder, Yvon Chouinard knows how to build trust and motivate staff at the same time. This surfer-leader makes sure that hanging above the receptionist's desk, surfing conditions, like wave size and water quality, are posted. And when surf's up, almost everyone, including pets, clears out and heads to the beach. Chouinard trusts that his employees will return to complete their work even more motivated than when they started!

their mistakes. They know the organization trusts that they'll correct the problem and do the right thing because it's the right thing to do. They don't get stuck or afraid. They know it all comes down to movement and momentum and that they've got to keep going forward to keep the respect and support of top management at all times. Respect the process," says Proffitt. "Hire the best people you can and then trust those people, or you'll wipe out!"

CREATIVITY AND TRUST TRUMP TECHNICALITIES

FOR EXAMPLE

MBSI has a strong and credible reputation as the most successful industry leader among medical billing companies in the nation. The reason? Its management staff and teams are known for exhibiting high levels of trust in the workplace, says one colleague.

Here you have an industry leader that could easily get locked down in the daily details of precision auditing, compliance coding, hospital practices, custom data analysis, and electronic submission of claims. But instead, leadership at MBSI encourages creativity and innovation, supported by mutual trust as one of its core leadership competencies.

"It's something I believe in strongly," says COO and president James V. Proffitt. Companies that succeed do so, in my opinion, because they exhibit high levels of trust in their people. I believe that innovation and positive change come from trust and that's when you get to see individual wins that lead to organizational wins—talk about motivating!"

How Trust Will Help Your Employees

"To really be able to help employees," says Proffitt, "they first have to trust your motives and believe in your advice. At that point, it's easy to discuss what's important, develop career plans, give constructive and honest feedback, memorialize action plans, and track progress via review sessions. Then, if you need to have the 'tough love' discussion, it's more likely to be accepted."

Motivation is partly based on a vision of hope—the hope for success from our efforts and for a better future for ourselves. In other words, *what life could be*. When we believe in the possibilities, a brighter tomorrow opens up.

We can find examples of this power of hope almost anywhere.

A Profound Message About Human Potential

In the popular and famously uplifting classic movie *Phenomenon*, the story of an ordinary man transformed by extraordinary events, George Malley (played by John Travolta) is knocked to the ground by a mysterious, blinding light. From this experience, George suddenly develops amazing and superhuman capabilities.

Throughout the movie, everyone, including George, assumes that the extraordinary talents he now possesses are surely the result of some supernatural power, perhaps a spell placed on him from outer space. The truth, however, is that George has a terminal brain tumor. The tumor, as it turns out, caused the bright flash of light George experienced. The real "phenomenon" was that George himself performed all of the amazing feats—reading and comprehending volumes of books in minutes and, therefore, learning at incredible speed everything from languages to medicine. In short, George maximized his own full potential.

This profound message about our untapped potential is poignantly expressed near the end of the movie in a conversation between George and a brain surgeon. The surgeon is trying desperately to convince George that, since he is going to die, he should let the doctors operate on his living brain, from which they can learn a great deal more about how he was able to accomplish so many amazing things. The doctor concludes, "You can be our greatest teacher. I can present you to the world."

Of course, the surgeon was completely missing the most obvious point. By simply living, George was already the greatest teacher—and he was proof of the extraordinary human potential that lies inside all of us.

George rejects the doctor's suggestion, eloquently telling him, "I am what everyone can be. I'm the possibility and anyone can get there. The human spirit—that's the challenge, that's the voyage, that's the expedition."

Finding True Hope over Great Odds

The spirit of the book you're now reading is *true hope*. It's the knowledge that our individual images of achievement, even over great odds, tap our deepest beliefs about our abilities and self-worth. We can all be more if we have hope. We can move mountains of doubt in others—and in ourselves. As George Malley said "We are the possibility and anyone can get there."

As a manager, one of the most important things you can do for your people is to give them hope or their *potential possibility*. This isn't just hope by itself, but hope that offers direction, believability, and genuine encouragement—hope with the belief that the future is going to be bright, no matter where everyone is at the moment.

> **Potential possibility**
> Latent ability that may or may not be developed.
> **KEY TERM**
> What's your potential? How do you know? Many people just assume. They tend to think of potential as something determined by birth.
> The most important part of this definition of potential is the clause "that may or may not be developed." Whatever your potential may be, you won't know unless you develop it. That's up to you.

When people have a good sense about their future, it reinforces their enthusiasm and commitment to the work in which they're involved. It says there's a payoff to the individual for doing well.

Trust Your Employees

Trust is an essential element in managing people and building a high-performing organization. It's the foundation on which all relationships are built.

According to Tom Peters, "Technique and technology are important. But adding trust is the issue of the decade." Peters suggests that managers must take both a "high-tech and high-trust"

> **Trust** Reliance on the integrity and abilities of a person.
> **KEY TERM**
> That's a basic definition. But the essence and value of trust are difficult to put into words, at least concisely. Trust involves faith, confidence, and hope. We tend to think of trust as being inspired by the person, but that's only part of trust.
> Consider these words by François de la Rochefoucauld: "The trust that we put in ourselves makes us feel trust in others." That's another thought every manager should place prominently on the office wall.

approach, putting the issue of trust at the top of the agenda and treating it like a "hard issue," not a "soft issue." If employees feel you don't trust them to do their jobs correctly and well, they'll be reluctant to do much without your approval. On the other hand, when they feel trusted, that you believe they'll do the right things well, they'll naturally want to do things well and be deserving of your trust.

Show Employees They're Worthy of Your Trust

When you put your trust in others, you're sending a strong message that says, "I think you're trustworthy." This tells people that you have faith in their ability and competence and you believe they've got what it takes to do the job. Trust is a prerequisite for building confidence in people.

Maybe you don't express your trust in employees very well—or at all. Maybe you assume your employees understand that you trust them. After all, you're not always hanging around them to make sure they don't make any mistakes. So they know you trust them, right?

Wrong! They know only that you don't have so little trust in them that you're going to go to great effort to supervise them closely. What reason do you give them to believe anything more than that?

Many managers don't talk about trust—or they use the word in limited contexts, often almost negatively. For example, "Now, Paul, I trust you to do this right" means "Don't screw up!" and "We're trusting you to do your best, Mary" really sends the message "We're not sure what's happening here, so we're just hoping that you can somehow work things out." These expressions of "trust" are unlikely to reassure Paul or Mary. So what do you do instead? Show your trust in employees by allowing them to think, ask questions, and make decisions. Those are expressions of trust employees can sense and believe.

Reinforcing Hope and Trust

Every organization depends on relationships, within and without. And relationships depend on trust. But that feeling must go in both directions. It's not enough for you to trust your employees. They've got to trust you as well.

Workers want to trust and believe in their managers. They want to believe that their managers are really looking out for their best interests.

Your people are your greatest resource. You may have hired them for their *aptitudes*, but the key to greater performance lies in their *attitudes*. The more you can do to build hope and trust in your employees, the more motivated they will be. Let's look at some specific ways you can do this throughout your organization.

The 12 Cornerstones for Building Hope and Trust in an Organization

1. Respect your followers. Forget about job titles and pay differences. Recognize the basic equality of all people. Respect is built on a mutual understanding that you and your employees all have a stake in the organization's future and success.

2. Watch how you say it. Cultivate a calm and considered approach. Voice tone is critical. Also, timing can be crucial: your words will be interpreted according to the context. How, when, and where you say something can actually be more important than the message itself.

3. Do what you say you're going to do. Be short on promises and long on fulfillment. Your credibility is at stake. Unfortunately, many managers say one thing and do another. Sure, you can't always do what you intend to do because life gets in the way. But sometimes it's easier to find excuses than to come through with results. Avoid that temptation. Use your position to build credibility among your employees and to increase their faith and hope in you and the organization.

4. Communicate openly. The best way for you to build trust is to communicate openly with your employees. Let people know what's going on! Make announcements in meetings, send send e-mails, Skype, Tweet, text, use bulletin boards, or publish a newsletter. Maybe you could even make a rap video you can show throughout the organization—Warren Buffett did it for GEICO and Herb Kelleher did it for Southwest Airlines. Be open and consistent. Share information as it becomes available and invite questions and comments from your employees.

5. Listen and don't argue. Listening speaks louder than words in conveying respect and trust. It says you care. Listening doesn't necessarily mean agreeing. Agree to disagree, if you must. And when you disagree, do so without being disagreeable. Maintain your respect for one another. If you don't understand or agree with someone, ask more questions. Find out where the other person is coming from. Be patient and considerate.

6. Avoid the zingers. Zingers, digs, or putdowns generally aren't funny. In fact, they may reveal insecurity and a lack of caring on your part. Be sensitive about your employees' feelings.

Don't Just Win, Succeed

As Robert Estabrook, former editor of *The Washington Post* editorial page, once noted, "He who has learned to disagree without being disagreeable has discovered the most valuable secret of a diplomat." But what is that secret?

If it can be summed up in a few words, it might be these three steps:

1. Rephrase the position or proposal you're questioning.
2. Go through each point and present your reasons for questioning each.
3. Try to transform these points into another position or proposal that you believe is better.

The purpose is not to win, but to arrive together at a better place. If you can get there from the other person's position or proposal, you're more likely to be able to bring him or her along more easily.

7. Point out the positive. Notice the good things about people and talk about them. That rewards their efforts and encourages them to try even harder.

8. Appreciate what others have to say. Show people that you value their perspectives—especially if they differ from yours. View a conversation not as a chance to express your views, but as an opportunity to find out how others think and feel. If you focus on asking rather than on telling, you'll be amazed at what you learn.

9. Acknowledge that trust is a mutual exchange. Don't expect others to trust you more than you trust them. If you treat people as if you're unsure of their trustworthiness—if you don't let them take on more responsibility, make decisions, or use authority—then how can you expect them to trust you in return? Trust flows both ways—and not necessarily better uphill. Remember the Golden Rule: *Do unto others as you would have others do unto you.* In other words, don't give what you don't want back.

10. Gradually increase trust. Trusting your employees doesn't happen overnight. Your trust in people builds over time and on the basis of their behaviors. Employees will gradually earn your trust when they do as they promise and follow up on their commitments. The more their behavior reassures you, the more you begin to trust them. You earn the trust of your employees the same way.

11. Be truthful with yourself. Do you believe in what you're conveying to others? Are you true to yourself, leading by example and doing the right thing in accordance with your values? You can't be a good manager if you're acting in ways that are inconsistent with who you are. In fact, you'll only be a poor model for your employees, inspiring them to wear masks of their own.

12. Show your human side. Share your mistakes, your hopes, and your dreams. Be down to earth and straightforward with people. Don't hide your mistakes or try to find excuses. Employees will respect and appreciate your honesty and your humanity.

The Benefits of a Trusting Organization

One of the benefits of building a trusting organization is that people in such a setting feel truly motivated and inspired to do the best they can each day. This level of trust is especially put to the test when there are no managers around.

A Moving Experience

A small but successful advertising firm had outgrown its location in downtown Dallas. In just three short years, the firm had expanded from 12 employees to over 40. Due to unavoidable circumstances, the agency had to vacate its site by April 30. Unfortunately, its new site in neighboring Plano would not be ready until June 15, maybe even as late as June 30.

> ### DON'T CUT CORNERS
> We've all known managers who have behaved inappropriately, cut ethical corners, and used others. That's bad and ineffective management.
>
> A managerial colleague once offered these words of advice: "Your people may not always be as good as you try to be, but you can be sure they're likely to be as bad as you allow yourself to be."
>
> As a manager, you assume a heavy burden. You've got to be open and honest about who you are, and always seek to improve. That's tough. But as this colleague summed it up, "Just be the person you'd like to have as your manager."

The firm's executives realized they'd be running a firm without offices for as long as six to eight weeks. The first question from the creative director was "How is this going to affect overall billings for those two months?" Another department manager was concerned about staff morale and attitude.

A team of VPs, department managers, and the president came together to decide on how to handle the situation. They agreed that it was a matter of trust. Their decision: everyone would work from home, with the exception of a skeleton crew who would remain on site to maintain the computer systems and a few diehards willing to cover the phones in the new building, which was still under construction and had no heating or air conditioning. The employees working at the two locations volunteered for those responsibilities; there was no griping or complaining.

> **ANOTHER PERSPECTIVE ON TRUST**
> Do you trust your employees? Do they trust you? Before you answer either of these questions, read what Douglas McGregor, author of *The Human Side of Enterprise*, says about trust: "Trust is the knowledge that you will not deliberately or accidentally, consciously or unconsciously, take unfair advantage of me. I can put my situation at the moment, my status, and self-esteem in this group, our relationship, my job, my career, even my life, in your hands with complete confidence."
> Do you and your employees have this kind of trust in each other?

What was the outcome of this seemingly difficult situation? These two months represented the largest billings in the history of the company! One employee credited the firm's leadership and its "positive thinking and belief in the people." Another employee stated, "They trusted us. We had to demonstrate we were worthy of that trust—and we did."

The firm turned a potentially disastrous situation into a positively outrageous, highly profitable one because the managers believed in—and trusted—the employees. Even if the profits had not been so healthy, there was certainly a success story here—in the victory of hope and trust.

When Trust Is Lost

Whenever we perceive an inequity between what we're putting into a relationship and what we're getting out of it, we lose some of our trust. That's true generally in our lives and perhaps particularly in the workplace. If workers perceive a balance between what they're giving and what they're receiving, their trust will be high. If they perceive an imbalance between the two, their trust will start to fall off.

Trust is largely a factor of *empowerment* (see Chapter 5). When you empower your employees, you show how much you trust them, giving them powerful reasons to trust you in return.

What happens when you don't empower your employees? Well, when you take away all the excuses for not empowering them, what's left is a lack of trust. Take a moment to reflect on your own actions as a manager. Are you guilty of any of the following behaviors that cause employees to lose trust?

Employees lose trust in you when:

- You say you'll empower them, but you find excuses not to.
- You deliberately instill fear and anxiety in them.
- You're manipulative.
- You fail to deliver on promises or you make empty promises.
- You inform the public about something before telling employees about it.
- You don't tell them what you expect from them.
- You give rewards that mean little or nothing to them.
- You're inaccessible and always behind closed doors.
- You delegate responsibility without authority.

Do any of these behaviors hit close to home for you? If so, what can you do to regain the trust of your employees?

Passion Turns Zero into a Hero—Teach Employees to Trust in Themselves

Teach your employees to turn their "zeros" into opportunities and to trust in their greater potential. You don't necessarily need to be an expert on a subject to deliver exceptional results. Sometimes you have to trust the process.

My friend, Mohamed Tohami, an effective motivational speaker in Cairo, Egypt, and bestselling author of *The Pharaohs' Code*, was interviewed for a position early in his career by an IT firm. While he wanted ultimately to be a speaker, he went into the technical interview with enthusiasm. The interviewer asked, "Can you deliver a time management course?"

"Of course I can," responded Tohami, even though he had zero experience in time management practices. He got the job, and spent the next two weeks reading, researching, and developing a two-day training program. "I worked on that course as if my life depended on it—because it did," states Tohami. "It was a golden opportunity that I simply couldn't let pass me by, the perfect chance to start my speaking career."

Tohami delivered the speech, and the results were so phenomenal that he was recommended for follow-up training sessions. He proved that having "zero" experience doesn't have to matter if you have energy and motivation to learn. "Pinpoint an area that you're truly passionate about," states Tohami. "Then put all your energy into studying that area until you know it inside out. Prepare and practice, and trust that one day, opportunity will knock on your door—and when it does, open that door and seize that opportunity with courage and passion. Give it everything you've got." What does this mean for management and motivation? If you can teach your employees to believe in their potential, and give them a chance to deliver on their passions, you open doorways to new successes and results.

For more motivational stories and helpful advice from Tohami, visit www.MotivationalTransformation.com.

Let Your Employees Run the Show

Let employees run the show? That suggestion strikes fear into the hearts of many managers. After all, if employees were running the show, what would managers do?

Managers too often forget how important trust is in an organization. Sure, they might talk about it. But then many behave in ways that show they really don't understand trust—or just don't care enough about it.

It's often a question of perception, of a difference in perspectives. What happens when you give your employees a project? Maybe you

> **SMART MANAGING**
>
> **SHOW YOUR TRUST**
>
> Give your employees what they need to do their jobs—tools, resources, support, and so on. Then give them the freedom to work with the commitment and passion of entrepreneurs. That's a great way to show you trust them!

intervene a little here and there. You might think of it as taking necessary precautions. But to your employees, it may seem like you really don't have enough faith in them to do it right on their own. Maybe you bring in outsiders to help out, thinking you'll give your employees some extra

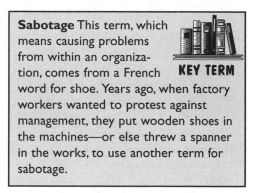

Sabotage This term, which means causing problems from within an organization, comes from a French **KEY TERM** word for shoe. Years ago, when factory workers wanted to protest against management, they put wooden shoes in the machines—or else threw a spanner in the works, to use another term for sabotage.

resources. But your employees may take it as evidence that you don't believe they'll get the job done.

What's missing in these, no doubt, common situations? Optimism and faith. You have to be optimistic about the final outcome and have faith that your people will do the job right. Otherwise you risk sabotaging the success of the project and undermining the confidence of your employees to do their jobs.

This sort of *sabotage* is rare now. In fact, the primary sabotage in organizations today is psychological—and it's often managers, not workers, who are guilty of hurting the organization from within.

You're a Guardian of the Organization's Values

It's probably not in your job description to be a "guardian of the organization's values." When you assumed your position as a manager, your boss probably didn't mention this part of your job—at least not in so many words. But you are indeed a guardian of the organization's values. This means you have responsibility for putting those values into the decisions you make and the actions you take.

We have repeatedly stressed the importance of integrity, of being true to yourself. You must be willing to stand by, live by, and work by your values. Employees want and need managers they can respect, not managers who are weak, who ride the political fences, and who lean whichever way everyone else seems to be leaning.

But what about the *values* of your *organization*? After all, you're not working for yourself. Employees learn about your organization's integrity and values by watching how *you* and its other leaders behave. In other words, how *you* behave says everything about what you value, as an individual and *as a representative of your organization*. If there are differences between your personal values and the values of your organization, you may need to make compromises. That's just being realistic. It's a question of how much "moral and emotional dissonance" you can accept. And only you can make that decision.

> **KEY TERM** **Value** This term, as it relates to organizational and personal behaviors, means what people feel is right, good, moral, appropriate, and important. Our behaviors—such as being truthful or, for some people, "looking out for #1"—reflect what we actually value, whether that's what we profess or not.

Whatever your particular situation, a basic fact stands out. When you establish congruence between individual values and organizational values, significant benefits can result. Because people are guided by their values, employees will often perform at their best when they can follow a set of core values and principles they understand and accept.

Values Create Loyalty and Trust

Anita Roddick, founder of the Body Shop and author of the book, *Body and Soul: Profits with Principles*, was a pioneer in stressing the importance of incorporating values into day-to-day business operations. The concept, known as "values-led leadership," is based on the idea that organizations have a responsibility to their people and to the society that makes their existence possible. The Golden Rule is a basic guide for such organizations.

Values-led management can produce a kind of loyalty and trust among employees and customers that most organizations only dream of. When employees feel they can really believe in the fundamental values and principles of the organization, when the managers live those values, they'll want to remain a part of the organization.

In values-led organizations, managers model the example and don't ask others to do anything they themselves wouldn't do. If you practice this "walk-the-talk" style of managing, your employees will naturally hold you in high esteem.

Think Globally, Act Locally

Maybe you're reading this chapter and agreeing with the idea and idealism of values-led management. You're interested in putting this principle into practice—but there's a problem: you don't control the entire organization. You're just a manager. What can you do?

"Think globally, act locally." This popular slogan makes good sense, not only for our environment but also for your workplace. You can change the big picture by starting small.

ROLE MODELS

To better understand values-led leadership, do some research on any of the following companies: Zappos, Burt's Bees, Clif Bar, The Body Shop, Ben & Jerry's, SAS, USAA, The Methodist Hospital System, Patagonia, Odwalla, Hewlett-Packard, Virgin Group, Ltd., Coca-Cola, McDonald's, Starbucks, Whole Foods Market, Marriott, Southwest Airlines, Hallmark, Levi Strauss, Blue Fish Clothing, Rhino Entertainment, St. Jude Children's Research Hospital, Nordstrom, May Clinic, Build-a-Bear Workshop, Boston Consulting Group, Intel, The Ritz-Carlton (Marriott International), and The Marcus Buckingham Company

Do what you can to lead your employees with positive values. Create an environment in which they feel privileged to make values matter, whatever happens elsewhere in the organization. Keep the spirit alive and support it so it grows and flourishes.

Don't worry about managers and employees outside your area. Let your results convince the other managers and let the other employees envy the atmosphere your employees enjoy. Set an example of values-led management. What you establish locally may spread to become global throughout the organization. But even if nobody else dares to take the values challenge, you'll at least be true to your beliefs and an inspiration to your employees. That alone will be worth the effort.

Inspiring Vision

This chapter began by discussing *what life could be*—the *vision* for a better and brighter future. As a manager, you're in charge of at least part of the big picture. Employees turn to *you* for further clarification and direction about the future of the organization and its values, principles, mission,

Vision We might best define this term as "seeing what isn't there—yet." Of **KEY TERM** course, a vision may mean very little unless you use it to inspire others to believe in it and commit to it.

When Walt Disney World opened, Walt Disney had already died. His wife was asked to speak on his behalf at the event. During her introduction, the man introducing her said, "Mrs. Disney, I just wish Walt could have seen this." She replied, "He did."

and goals. Create a vision that you can *share* with your people. If you have a vision and don't share it, you lose a powerful opportunity to influence your employees and help them find greater motivation in their work.

Think about how many successful companies are the result of the early vision of their leaders, like Walt Disney, Bill Gates, Oprah Winfrey, Sir Richard Branson, Howard Schultz of Starbucks, and Marcus Buckingham. These pioneers would not have been able to realize their dreams had they not shared those dreams with the people around them.

Light the Way and Fire People Up!

Employees won't have hope and trust if they don't know where the organization is headed. So it makes sense to share your vision with them to get their input on the vision you have for the future of the organization, or even for your department or group. Sharing a vision is a great way to positively influence your employees' motivation.

Somebody once said, "If we are to light the way, then we are going to have to set ourselves on fire." In other words, you have to show people what you feel burning within.

Realizing your vision may be a big project, but you can manage it in small ways. Encourage your employees to contribute their ideas. Involve them in creating your vision. Discuss what changes you see for the future and how everyone as a team can plan and work to make those changes happen.

Be certain that your vision aligns with the larger goals of the organization—your boss, a higher-level division, corporate headquarters. What are the organization's principles, values, and core beliefs? How can you develop your vision within that context? (If there's a discrepancy between the principles, values, and beliefs on paper and in practice, choose those that seem most realistic or most important for your department. Don't try to sell your employees something you don't buy yourself—and don't try to change the organization overnight.)

Once you develop that vision, then pursue it. Get everyone moving together, trusting in each other and committing to the vision. Share every success as a step toward achieving that vision. Success always reinforces motivation.

Manager's Checklist for Chapter 6

☑ Motivation is partly based on our hope for success from our efforts and for a better future.

☑ Hire the best, trust your people, or you may wipe out!

☑ Building trust means that you have to be out in front of your employees.

☑ Trust is essential for managing people and promoting better performance. It's the foundation for all relationships and a great source of motivation and inspiration. Without trust and respect, we run our organizations on wishes and fears.

☑ When you empower your employees, you show how much you trust them and you give them reason to trust you. Let them run the show. Be optimistic about the outcome and show faith that your people will do the job right.

☑ As a manager, you must be a guardian of your organization's values. You must live by those values and your own personal values. Employees often perform best when they can follow values and principles they understand and accept (and they learn about your organization's values and principles from you).

☑ Values-led management produces loyalty and trust among employees. The managers set the example and practice a "walk-the-talk" style of leadership.

☑ Go from zero to hero and trust your inner voice of wisdom and talents.

☑ Share your vision of the future with your employees so they feel hope and trust and a greater sense of motivation.

Fun and Motivation = Profits and Productivity

Fun Is an Organizational Strategy That Pays Big Benefits

E mployees who are having fun at work might well be exhibiting the single most important trait of highly effective and successful organizations.

We know from both qualitative and quantitative data that "fun at work" doesn't have to be an oxymoron. There's a direct correlation between fun on the job and employee productivity, creativity, morale, satisfaction, and, most of all, retention—not to mention greater customer satisfaction and a host of other benefits. In other words, people in this kind of environment come to see work as a place to fulfill many needs, reinforcing their motivation to perform at a high level.

In a work environment that encourages fun, employees have:

- Lots of energy
- Greater self-esteem
- Enthusiasm for their work
- Team spirit
- Sustainable motivation
- Positive attitudes that drive better behavior and better choices

You can certainly train people to do just about anything. But the key to real success—and to motivated employees—is having people who really *want* to do their jobs and who love to come to work. These people enliven the workplace and energize their coworkers. That's the difference having fun at work can make.

Humor is all about taking life less seriously. When we incorporate humor and fun—both natural human behaviors—into our lives, we automatically decrease tension, build confidence, and make life a little easier overall. There's little else that will make a person feel as good as a laugh.

The Aussie Who Motivates Leaders with FUN!

Amanda Gore is a fabulously fun Aussie. She's also a respected physical therapist with a major in psychology. Gore is a top-rated inspirational and motivational author and keynoter who speaks on how emotional intelligence makes us more successful at work and at home. Amanda has spent most of her life dedicated to helping people better connect to their heart with their head! See Gore in action in her videos featured at AmandaGore.com. Having done so, you will almost instantly begin to transform as a more motivated manager. Here you will find lots of advice and free information on how to realize your individual balance, live longer, feel happier, bust your stress, and be a better, stronger, and happier manager and leader overall.

Get Motivated and Try Endorphins: The Body's Natural Happy Drug!

"Laughter really is the best medicine," says Gore. "Recent studies show that people can boost their immune systems with laughter. Laughter stimulates the release of hormones called endorphins into your bloodstream and these chemicals make you feel good."

"Endorphins are actually the body's natural 'happy drugs,'" Gore explains. Recognized some years ago by scientist Candace Pert, endorphins are powerful drugs and often are much better at pain relief than anything scientists can synthetically manufacture.

"We humans can produce them at will," says Gore. "All we have to do is exercise, or fall in love, or laugh a lot, or draw a smiley face on our finger (the index finger is best!) and wave it at people accompanied with a high pitched 'hello' and there will be endorphins everywhere, flooding our brains!"

AMANDA RECOMMENDS MANAGERS HAVE SOME FUN!

TOOLS

"If we aren't responsible for our own fun, nobody else will be," says Gore. "So sometimes we just have to break out, let go, and be silly, because if we don't, the alternative may be a heart attack or sickness. If we stay angry, stressed, and intense, we can't manufacture the endorphins we need to feel good and bust our stress. But worse than that, you're probably making yourself sick! So don't be an energy sucker! In laughing and letting go as a manager, you help others to release endorphins and build their energy, too!"

With this simple exercise as an icebreaker in meetings, you can release everyone's endorphins and create a better mood in the workplace.

Ready, Steady, Go! Team Exercise

OK, hold up your index finger, look for your new best friend (whoever is sitting next to you), and draw a smile with two dots on their finger. Together you have created endorphins and can change your day with your own natural energy. Ready, steady, go! Feel the energy build, burst out of your seat, wave your finger and say "hello" to at least 10 people! Feel how the energy in the room goes up and how the mood shifts to being lighter, happier, and less stressful in just minutes.

Taking Motivation and Happiness to the Next Level

Recently Amanda Gore launched an international effort called "The Joy Project." The Joy Project is all about creating a Global Joy Community wherever you work or live. As Amanda says in her bestselling book, *The Gospel of Joy,* joy is bigger than happiness, which is just a small part of the iceberg. Most of us think we will be happy when we have something that we don't have now. Which means we're hardly ever happy!

But we're born with the capacity to be joyful. To achieve that, we don't need anything else or anyone's permission. We can be joyful all the time. It's a choice and it takes work. And it can be brought to the workplace to create better, happier, more productive, and profitable environments.

Managers can learn more about this worldwide phenomenon by visiting TheJoyProject.com where you can take advantage of lots of tools and ideas to achieve greater joy in your organization, among your colleagues, and in your personal life!

Watch Amanda's video about this exciting Global Joy Community that she's building and learn how you, too, can be part of it. There you'll also find JoyU Online Learning Programs and much more.

Physiological Benefits of Humor

The late Norman Cousins, editor of the now defunct but once popular magazine, *Saturday Review*, and author of the timeless book *Anatomy of an Illness*, referred to laughter as one of the "healing powers of nature." Cousins used humor and laughter as medicine in combating his own life-threatening illness. He won the battle and lived a long life.

So when we discuss fun and humor at work, it's important to look at the physiological benefits for you and your employees.

What Fun Does for Our Minds and Bodies

Fun, laughter, humor—they're all cleansing. They unite us with everyone else who is having fun. They can make it nearly impossible to feel lonely or left out. When we share a laugh, we enjoy the laugh—but we also feel the sharing.

Humor helps us put things into perspective. When you encourage people to have a sense of humor about their work, it forces them to take a step back from the situation at hand. When they do that, they can usually see more clearly and in more detail everything surrounding the situation.

Fun Is Holistic

Fun is motivating because of the pleasure it creates. It stimulates the pituitary gland, which produces endorphins and enkephalins, as Amanda Gore writes about. These are natural painkillers that are 100 times more powerful than morphine! So when employees or managers are feeling down, stressed, tired, or just not in the mood to work up to their abilities, a laugh can make a big difference.

Fun: An Effective Organizational Strategy

Many organizations—including Southwest Airlines, Zappos, Starbucks, and Ben & Jerry's—use fun at work as an organizational strategy. Fun has become a strategic weapon to motivate employees and their managers to achieve extraordinary results and build strong, resilient organizational cultures—not to mention big profits. Organizations that instill fun in the workplace are laughing all the way to the bank!

Zappos Integrates Work Into Life. Zappos' management in fact specifically targets hires whom they feel they would want to hang out with after

---

TEN CHARACTERISTICS OF FUN

SMART

1. Humor busts stress and tension.
2. Fun improves communication and helps others to lighten up.
3. Fun eases conflicts and disagreements.
4. Laughter can help us survive in good times and bad times.

MANAGING

5. Laughing at yourself is the highest form of humor.
6. Laughter has a natural healing power and positive energy.
7. Humor helps lighten the load all of us carry every day.
8. Fun unites people and helps us embrace differences with a sense of humor.
9. Fun breaks up boredom and fatigue. It's a much-needed kick in the attitude.
10. Fun creates and grows positive energy and lively synergy.

---

work. In its early days, some of the key employees even lived together in a building that founder Tony Hsieh rented. They integrated work into life, and vice versa—often congregating around the clock for meals, events, leisure, and planning sessions. Even the language that Hsieh uses in his corporate memos incorporates an element of fun. He talks in his book *Delivering Happiness* about how he discovered through his successes and failures that despite logical convention that would state otherwise, money wasn't his motivator. Instead, the ability to act creatively and enjoy his work experience is what drove him. He brings these philosophies into the corporate culture at Zappos. The result? Zappos went from almost zero sales in 1999, to more than $1 billion in sales in 2008 (two years ahead of their goal).

Clif Bar Values Nonwork Life, Too. Similarly, Clif Bar values its employees and their nonwork lives. Corporate policy allows employees to bring their children or even dogs to work. The company maintains an on-site fitness program, and even offers a concierge service to help employees with daytime errands. Employees are also permitted to take up to three months of paid time off after they have worked there for seven years.

When workers are having fun, they're energized and motivated. When they're energized and motivated, they perform better. Translation: fun influences behaviors and is an effective formula for success.

We're not talking about making work a place to play or have fun for the sake of fun. But work rarely needs to be as serious as many people

TRICKS OF THE TRADE

Fun and the Bottom Line

Do you want to reduce absenteeism, promote greater job satisfaction, boost employee performance, increase productivity, and suffer less downtime? Of course! But how? By encouraging fun. These are among the bottom-line benefits of a fun work environment.

make it. Why should employees suppress their sense of humor on the job? That undermines their motivation because it makes them less human. The idea here is to allow people to feel more comfortable and to make the workplace more enjoyable.

Using Humor to Get Your Point Across

Managers at Southwest Airlines encourage employees to use humor to get their messages across. If you've ever flown the fun-in-the-sky carrier, you've probably heard a creative and unique flight attendant rendition of the emergency safety procedures, which are typically considered (on other airlines) to be a ho-hum routine. Here are some excerpts:

- As the song goes, there might be 50 ways to leave your lover, but there are only six ways to leave this aircraft.
- In the event of a water evacuation, your bottom—your seat bottom, that is—can be used as a flotation device.
- Those of you who wish to smoke will be asked to step out to our lounge on the wing, where you can enjoy our feature movie presentation, *Gone with the Wind.*

Does this sound like fun and games? Yes. But Southwest receives thousands of letters from happy and loyal customers as a result. And you can bet that on this airline, unlike many others, passengers are paying close attention to the emergency procedures and remembering everything! Isn't that the point?

Of course. The difference is, here's a company using creative humor to make the point. What a novel idea!

Any CEO Who Wears a Swimming Pool to Work Is Cool

A market leader in providing nonstandard auto insurance, Progressive Insurance is also a leader when it comes to profiting from a fun culture. According to the company's zany leaders, people spend more time at work than anywhere else—and life's too short to not enjoy what you're doing. The organization's belief is that a creative and stimulating work environment is motivation at its finest because it enhances individual energy and on-the-job satisfaction.

The atmosphere at Progressive promotes having fun at work so that employees will work harder and achieve greater results. One year,

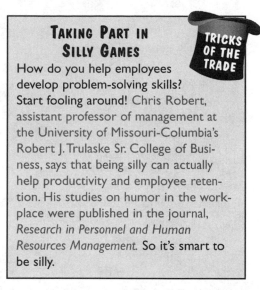

TAKING PART IN SILLY GAMES

How do you help employees develop problem-solving skills? Start fooling around! Chris Robert, assistant professor of management at the University of Missouri-Columbia's Robert J. Trulaske Sr. College of Business, says that being silly can actually help productivity and employee retention. His studies on humor in the workplace were published in the journal, *Research in Personnel and Human Resources Management.* So it's smart to be silly.

founder, then CEO, now chairman, Peter B. Lewis, showed up at the company's traditionally "outrageous" Halloween event wearing a swimming pool! Other executives have dressed as gangsters, robots, rock stars, a large box of crayons—even a six-pack of beer!

Progressive continues to be excited about its dedicated employees who work hard—not to mention record-breaking profits! It appears there's something to this fun stuff after all.

Making Work More Enjoyable

You don't have to wear costumes and do comedy routines to make your work environment more enjoyable. You can work wonders by simply dropping conventional "costumes" and traditional work routines.

What's Hot and What's Not

What's working at work these days and what's being retired? How can you improve your little corner of the jungle? Here are some guidelines:

I called these lists "What's Hot" and "What's Not," but I'm not really trying to promote fads. The "hot" items are simply more effective than the "not" items at boosting motivation and productivity. They work because they're real.

What's Hot	What's Not
Respect and honor everyone different than ourselves	Fear and resentment of others
Employee Resource and Affinity Groups	Diversity like we practiced it a decade ago
Managers who manage relationships first	Managers who try to manage people's lives
Casual attire	Suits and pantyhose
Skechers, Nikes and other comfortable shoes	High heels and wing tips
Managers who ride bicycles and Harleys	Managers who ride in limos
Managing "green" and respecting the planet	Wasting energy
Innovative and creative thinking	Doing things the same old way
Hugs and fist bumps	Handshakes only
Empowerment	Micro-management
Turbo-charged teams	Individual superstars
Celebrating mistakes	Punishment for mistakes
Flexibility	Strict corporate policies
Leaders	Bosses
Common sense and good judgment	Corporate mandates and lots of policies
"Friending" coworkers on Facebook	Gossip
Silly contests	Rigidity

Fundamentals of Humor

Maybe you're convinced that it's good business to loosen up and to encourage your employees to enjoy their work. Great!

But what if you just don't know how to go about it? Here are some tips to help get you started:

1. Laugh with people, not at them. And don't be afraid to laugh at yourself.
2. Lighten up. Don't take yourself too seriously.
3. Laugh out loud and you'll live out loud.
4. Think with a sense of humor. Humor is a leadership competency that works.

SECOND CITY COMEDY THEATRE BRINGS FUN TO MANAGEMENT

SMART

MANAGING

If there is anything that Sarah Finch learned from her years as an actor trainer, including five years of work with Second City Communications, the corporate arm of the Second City comedy theatre, it's that people are just waiting for permission to have fun and play.

Sarah says that the ability of managers to learn, grow relationships, and improve motivation can be increased just by being willing to laugh with each other.

Using secrets from theatre and improvisation, Sarah now helps managers and other groups use the secrets of theatre and improvisation to make managing and learning in the workplace fun—whether managers are building teams, developing leaders, or helping individuals improve their own presentation or facilitation skills.

Catch Sarah's motivational training techniques at international conferences, like the annual American Society for Training and Development International Conference and Exposition (ASTD ICE), where her closing keynote address is one of the most popular and entertaining. Sarah can be found on the speaking circuit promoting her message of fun and entertaining management techniques and innovative learning skills. Google Sarah or e-mail her at sarahfinch3@gmail.com.

---

5. Adopt a fun and playful attitude about life and work.
6. Plan to have a good time—anticipate good things.
7. Be spontaneous—go with the flow. Don't make things harder than they need to be.
8. Help others see the lighter side of things.
9. Be outrageous—innovate and create every single day.

Want more help? Check out *301 Ways to Have Fun at Work* by Dave Hemsath and Leslie Yerkes.

If you follow these nine tips—which for some managers may be more of a nine-step program to recover from a serious addiction ... to being serious—you probably won't need any more guidelines. After all, having fun will become natural.

How to Inspire Fun in Your Employees

Work is not necessarily the price we pay to earn a living. It can be just the opposite, an enjoyable part of living. We should try to do what we love every day.

FUN SUGGESTIONS

TOOLS

Want to improve your work environment and put more fun in your functions? You've probably got the best resources all around you. That's right: your employees. Put up a box for "fun suggestions"—maybe just a shoebox decorated with colorful paper and crayons. If someone makes a simple suggestion, try it. If there's something more involved, put the suggestion to a vote. This is "bottom-up" improvement at its best.

Of course, we all have to do things we would rather not do. That's life. But we can keep our motivation up when we include in our daily work the things that consistently bring us joy.

As Mark Twain said, "The secret of success is making your vocation your vacation." Or in the words of the popular saying, "Choose a job you love and you will never have to work a day in your life."

Sure, easy for them to say. But you're a manager. What can you do? Well, Twain probably could have come up with some suggestions for you, such as the following:

- Be a role model for fun. Show how to have fun and still work hard.
- Set up some creativity sessions to help employees and managers learn how to think outside the box.
- Innovate! It can be fun to find better, cheaper, faster ways of doing things.
- Make up silly titles to go with new business cards, such as "Big Cheese."
- Motivate employees with personal thanks and public praise.
- Start a list of fundamentals for doing business in the workplace.

TRICKS OF THE TRADE

GETTING THE FUN STARTED

Start small in your efforts to create a more fun work environment. For example:

- If you find a funny comic or article in the newspaper, post it outside your office door.
- If you've got a young child, niece or nephew, or neighbor, a crayon drawing makes great art for any decor.
- When you send out your next memo, write it in a lighthearted fashion. Don't be any more serious than the situation requires.
- Begin your next meeting with a quote from a famous "philosopher," such as Scott Adams (Dilbert) or Gary Larson (The Far Side).

- Invite an employee with a great sense of humor to be "in charge of fun."
- Give unexpected gifts.
- Find the humor in every situation.
- Follow your intuition and be spontaneous.
- Share good news and funny moments.

These suggestions might be summed up simply in the following advice: Be human and find ways to enjoy what you're doing. Share the good feelings with your employees and encourage them to share their enjoyment.

Follow the Leaders

This suggestion may sound serious, even sinister, but you

PLAY AND STAY TOGETHER **SMART**

MANAGING

The company that plays together, stays together! That's a quote you might want to put on your office wall ... and maybe post conspicuously around your work area. Then be sure you make fun part of your way of managing. Not just because it makes work more enjoyable, but because it also can, in the right spirit, improve employee commitment, motivation, and performance.

might also consider engaging in a little corporate intelligence. Yes, be a "spy"! Study "fun" organizations and see what you can learn. Buy books about them, clip and save articles about them, check out information about them on the Internet, or even pay them a visit. Here are a few "fun organizations" that I recommend:

The Boston Beer Company	BestBuy
OWN (Oprah Winfrey Network)	Apple
Red Bull London	Think Geek.com
Google	Men's Wearhouse
SAS	Virgin Group, Ltd.
Southwest Airlines	Ben & Jerry's
Facebook	Disney
Netflix	Progressive Insurance
Marriott International	Pixar
Nordstrom	DreamWorks Animation SKG
MedAmerica Billing Services	AFLAC
General Mills	Whole Foods

Finding "fun companies" in your area might be as easy as checking out the local newspaper or business magazine.

Manager's Checklist for Chapter 7

☑ The single most important trait of highly effective and successful organizations is that their employees have fun at work. There's a direct correlation between fun on the job and employee motivation, productivity, creativity, morale, satisfaction, and retention. Also, when employees have fun on the job, it generally translates into greater customer satisfaction.

☑ Employees in a fun work environment have more energy, greater self-confidence, enthusiasm for their work, team spirit, positive attitudes, and sustainable motivation.

☑ Fun is an organizational strategy at some companies (one that's paying big benefits). You can learn a lot from these companies.

☑ You can make your work environment more fun by simply dropping conventional "costumes" and traditional work routines.

☑ Be human and find ways to enjoy what you're doing. Share the good feelings with your employees and encourage them to share their enjoyment.

☑ Take the workplace to a higher level—find joy, not just happiness.

Attacking the De-Motivators

Put the Kibosh on Whatever Brings Your Organization Down

This book is full of tools, tips, guidelines, and lists to help you positively influence the motivation of your employees. But let's face it. We live in demanding and increasingly negative times. No matter how supportive, motivating, or encouraging you may be as a manager, you're no doubt constantly facing circumstances that negatively influence the motivation of your employees. We call these the *de-motivators*. They're factors that disintegrate optimism, faith, and a positive outlook among your employees.

How do you build and maintain hope in the midst of influences that threaten to de-motivate? You attack the de-motivators.

By putting your energy into what you *can* do, rather than dwelling on de-motivating circumstances and making their effects worse, you'll be better able to combat doom and gloom and confront the adversity that negatively affects the motivation of your employees.

Shooing Away the "Attitude Vultures"

As a manager, keeping a solid gold attitude is crucial because what a manager exudes toward employees in the way of joy and enthusiasm for the tasks at hand is returned by employees in the form of work ethic, appreciation, respect, and overall engagement. Employees then pass that attitude on to customers, clients, and vendors.

119

KEY TERMS

De-motivators Factors that deflate the motivation bubble. They can be events, management decisions, disappointments, a lack of praise and rewards, and so on.

Attitude vultures These are the things that prey on one's best attitude by wearing down morale and making employees feel like their energy and efforts have been pecked by wild birds.

Sam Glenn, speaker and author of *A Kick in the Attitude*, says that for a team to perform optimally, a manager must keep the "attitude vultures" at bay. Just like vultures who prey on animals who may be tired, wounded, or looking vulnerable with a sideways limp, attitude vultures can sneak up and erode a team's efforts—leaving them stranded in the forest with no support network or exit strategy, and no ability to perform.

Fending off the attitude vultures requires not only keeping one's own attitude healthy and strong, but also fostering an environment wherein the employees are able to withstand attack from negative influences.

Glenn lists the following examples of attitude vultures that can sap morale and derail employees' efforts:

- Anger
- Laziness
- Fear
- Self-doubt
- Inflexibility
- Misplaced priorities
- Depressing the "fun factor"
- Defensiveness
- Judging others
- Hatred

What happens when one of these vultures takes over? Let's take anger, for example. An employee who exhibits anger toward a manager, task, coworker, or client may show it by stewing, being distracted, gossiping, or even lashing out verbally at those around her. This can lead to loss of morale, customers, and profit.

What about a loss of fun? Who would have thought that not having fun would kill productivity? Glenn believes that "terminal professional-

> ### FOSTERING FUN   SMART
>
> Want to foster more fun in the workplace? Follow these tips from
> Sam Glenn: MANAGING
>
> - Keep fun simple, like going to lunch with your team, perhaps
>   somewhere new—like the zoo!
> - Establish a fun committee to plan activities like recipe swapping, baby
>   picture sharing, etc.
> - Create a humor bulletin board with positive quotes, cartoons, jokes, or
>   ideas.
> - Kick off your meetings with fun and inspirational training DVDs.
> - Hold contests with simple or silly prizes.
> - Give staff Play-Doh for their desks.
> - Have a snack break—food is always fun!

ism" is risky to a company because it causes employees to become like prunes at work—all dried up with no real juice to get things rolling.

Managers who heighten awareness of internal vultures will prevent their employees from lying in the hills and getting pecked to bits. Addressing attitude vultures before they arise is the best way to avoid chaos, and keep your employees thriving. How can attitude vultures be shooed away? By fostering a healthy workplace. Here are a few ways that employees' attitudes can be kept strong enough to withstand any crazy birds that might attack:

- Hold regular meetings to go over team goals and get feedback from employees.
- Offer incentives to employees for meeting milestones.
- Share about upcoming changes to negate fear.
- Offer praise for work that is well done and celebrate victories.
- Find out what motivates each person on your team.
- Care about employees beyond the workplace, by learning about their lives, preferences, and goals.
- Don't feed gossip.
- Foster physical and mental health to model a strong attitude and exhibit sound leadership.

If you can follow these tips, you'll watch those vultures flapping their wings and flying south, as they will realize there is no wounded meat in your company!

Sam Glenn (also known as "The Attitude Guy") heads up "Go Positive University," where I've greatly enjoyed serving as a virtual professor of motivation and inspiration. Check it out at SamGlenn.com.

You Can Motivate or De-Motivate

As a manager, you have a tremendous responsibility to your employees. You directly or indirectly impact their self-confidence, their desires, their long-term interests, and their overall ability to love what they do for a living. That's a lot of pressure on you to get it right.

You're not responsible for protecting your employees against all the "downs" of life. But you should certainly want to help minimize the de-motivating effects with respect to the workplace. That's just a fundamental part of being an effective manager.

We've all had experiences that have undermined or even destroyed our motivation, at least for a while. For many of us, this de-motivation may have occurred at an early age, when we lost interest in something or in improving ourselves. Consider the following situation, which shows how one event can significantly hurt motivation.

A De-Motivating Experience

When Sara entered the seventh grade, she enrolled in a beginner's art class after school at the YWCA. The class was taught by a retired school teacher, Mrs. Cummings, who loved art and painting. Her love for art immediately rubbed off on her students. They, too, fell in love with art.

Sara's parents were thrilled to see what art class had done for their daughter. They often commented on how Sara would return home from her class with Mrs. Cummings each week with a big smile on her face. Sara would share with her parents her teacher's constant praise and support for her artwork.

To support Sara's interest, Sara's parents would often frame and hang a painting or drawing Sara had brought home. When the art classes came to an end, Sara decided to sign up for more art classes when she started the eighth grade.

And so she did. She signed up for two classes and even thought ahead about majoring in art in college. Sara loved drawing and painting—and it had all started with Mrs. Cummings.

Both of Sara's art classes in the eighth grade were taught by the head of the art department at her middle school. The teacher graded every one of Sara's drawings and paintings according to textbook definitions of "artistic" value, with little regard for Sara's love for what she was doing.

It wasn't long before Sara was going home from school bitter and angry. Soon she began to lose all interest in art. A month later, she dropped out of both art classes.

The Decline and Death of Motivation on the Job

Isn't this experience typical of what we sometimes see at work? We start to grade and assess people, to pass judgment on them and form opinions of them, and soon we lose sight of why they were drawn to do what they do in the first place. We completely cut off any opportunity for improvement—or motivation. The damage can be horrendous. Bear in mind at all times that every employee is an *individual*. Each one is different.

Performance Reviews Can Be De-Motivating

Performance reviews can be a valuable source of corrective and positive feedback for employees. They can help employees measure their progress toward established criteria and outcomes.

But they can also be devastating if you simply use them as report cards, to sum up an employee and objectify him or her. Rating systems such as these are poor substitutes for good management and leadership.

To build a truly motivating and motivated organization, you need to lead, not simply grade the performance of your employees. Performance reviews alone will hurt your efforts at motivating, especially when the truly important issues revolve around teamwork, cooperation, desire, personal interests, and goal-setting.

A Deadly Disease According to Deming

According to Dr. W. Edwards Deming, a founder of the quality movement, there are several deadly "diseases" that can keep people from improving. One of those dreaded diseases is *the evaluation of performance, merit ratings, or annual reviews*.

This disease can eventually kill the motivation of the people in the organization. Why? There are two primary reasons. One is that most performance appraisals are subjective, so employees tend to view them as judgmental. Two, performance appraisals focus on the individual employee, which ignores the importance of interrelationships in most workplaces. Since performance appraisals often seem unfair and unrealistic, they break down the trust between those being appraised and those doing the appraising.

In essence, that's why Deming suggested doing away with them. The remedy, according to Deming, is to replace performance reviews with leadership: managers should constantly improve the processes, not simply evaluate the employees.

This approach requires that you, as a manager, assume the responsibilities of *leading* your employees, not just measuring their progress every year. If you rely solely on annual ratings of your employees, you're encouraging the disease of de-motivation.

Fighting De-Motivators

There are hundreds of ways to bring down the morale of an organization—and therefore have a negative impact on employee motivation. But there are also four specific steps you can take to build organizational strength so that your employees can better handle de-motivating situations:

1. Hire the best.
2. Retain the best.
3. Give employees honest feedback, praise, and encouragement.
4. Build employees' confidence.

Step 1. Hire the Best

The best way to counter de-motivation is to prevent it. Sometimes the problem is with the people you hire. There are people who tend to get de-motivated easily. There are also people who undermine the motivation of others by spreading a feeling of hopelessness and apathy.

You can't always help people overcome their psychological issues. It's far wiser to try not to hire these people—to put your efforts into screening out candidates who seem likely to suffer from motivation problems.

A bad hire hurts the organization, the new hire, the other employees,

---

KNOW A BAD DOG FROM A SAD DOG

"Don't assume that a sad dog is a bad dog." These words from a dog lover make sense for managers as well.

Some dogs are just bad: maybe it's natural, maybe it's from experiences. A bad dog is unlikely to change, unless you're willing to commit a lot of time and effort to bring out whatever good lies inside. Those dogs will turn on you and can bring out the worst in other dogs.

But some sad dogs are just the victims of their circumstances. They respond positively to good treatment and will give everything they've got if you give them a chance.

There's a big difference between a bad dog and a sad dog. Be sensitive to that difference.

---

and you! When there are a lot of wrong people in the wrong jobs, the malady multiplies and you have a disease. This disease can poison other employees and hurt the entire organization. It can also undermine your managerial well-being—and possibly even kill your career.

HIRING FOR THE BEST FIT

Here are a few strategies you can use to hire for the best fit:

- Know what the job requires, in terms of skills and personality.
- Screen each candidate thoroughly. Get a good sense of his or her personality. This takes more time and energy, but it's worth the investment.
- Develop interviewing techniques that focus not only on the job, but also on your organization's culture.
- Get second opinions about the candidates. Invite a few employees to participate in part of the interviewing. Then have them share their impressions with you.
- Don't oversell the organization—e.g., compensation, benefits, or career opportunities.
- Check each candidate's references.

Best Practices in Hiring

At many of the world's top companies, managers take extraordinary pains to attract and hire employees who will further strengthen the organization. Here are some world-class examples of how it's being done.

Rosenbluth International tests people for "niceness." This well-known and highly successful travel management company takes a unique approach to hiring "nice" people. Its credo: you can teach people almost anything, but you can't teach them to be nice. This philosophy certainly goes along with the "hire for attitude, train for skill" belief characterizing many organizations.

Rosenbluth uses a few unique methods to evaluate job candidates. One approach is to ask the applicant to play a trial game of softball with the company team. The company feels this gives everyone a pretty good sense of the candidate's manner, team spirit, and rapport.

Then there are the potential executive hires, who are often flown to Rosenbluth's ranch in North Dakota so that they can work as ranch hands. The candidates are asked to fix fences and even drive cattle! How well they perform these tasks doesn't matter one bit. What matters to Rosenbluth recruiters is one thing: was the candidate pleasant and nice while doing the tasks? The answer had better be "yes" to land an executive position with the $3.5 billion company.

BE CAREFUL WHEN YOU GET PHYSICAL

CAUTION If you decide to use tests that involve physical abilities that are not essential for the job responsibilities—such as would be involved in playing softball or working on a ranch—be careful not to discriminate against candidates for whom such activities are difficult or impossible.

The key here is to bring in people with good attitudes, not reject people who can't hit a softball or rope a steer or do other physical activities unrelated to the job.

The interviewing teams at W.L. Gore and Associates stress fitting into their *very unstructured* culture. The Newark, Delaware, company—which produces dental floss, medical implants, and the famous Gore-Tex fabric—uses a team of interviewers. To get a job, a candidate must answer questions centered on the company's nontraditional culture, where there are no organizational charts or titles and pay raises are based on the results of a biannual peer review.

W.L. Gore is also adamant about checking references. Managers sometimes check as many as 10 references for a candidate, speaking not only to former bosses and supervisors, but also to peers and subordinates.

Federal Express checks for "the right stuff" by assessing a candidate's leadership dimensions. Candidates for managerial positions are evaluated on judgment and decision-making ability, flexibility, and dependability. In addition, FedEx job candidates might well be asked to stand and deliver a five-minute speech on some aspect of the business. The purpose: to see if candidates can think on their feet.

This should give you some ideas about how managers hire at some companies. Maybe your own organization is not world-class (yet!). But you certainly can learn from what others are doing and improve how you interview and screen job candidates.

Whatever systems and processes you develop for hiring, it's crucial to make sure the personality of a candidate fits the job and your environment. If you have reason to believe that the candidate might not be properly motivated to perform up to your expectations, avoid potential problems and don't hire that candidate. There's rarely a candidate with such great skills and experience that you should even consider overlooking motivation that could be a problem.

Step 2. Retain the Best

Hiring the best people (those who are highly motivated and perform well) is one thing. Retaining them is another.

Not long ago, managers were encouraging employees to take early retirement and severance packages. How things have changed! Today, managers are eager to retain good employees. When you invest a lot in your employees, you create a valuable asset, and you naturally want to hold onto them—and keep them motivated.

What does it take to retain and maintain those employees? It's not just about money, titles, or shareholder value. (And you may not have much power to control those aspects.) It's also a matter of creating an environment where your employees feel right—a culture that suits them.

Creating an Environment Where Your Employees Feel Right

Smart managers are recognizing the competitive value of having good employees who feel motivated to excel.

HR directors now worry whether the best employees are truly happy in their jobs and engaged to produce. That's an important concern for any organization—and any manager. The question is, to what extent are you willing to change your environment to keep your best workers? That's a tough decision. Here are a few alternatives for you to consider.

Why Employees Stay

Employees have many reasons for staying with a job. To retain their employees, some companies find innovative ways to apply what researchers such as Abraham Maslow (Chapter 2) have revealed about human nature and our needs. Here are just two examples of retention practices that work.

At Medtronic, a medical products company in Minneapolis that makes half of the heart pacemakers in the world, employees are motivated daily by a sense of purpose—helping people get well. The company's mantra: "To alleviate pain, restore health, and extend life." As an extra motivational boost for employees, patients are invited to an annual holiday party at the company and asked to tell how Medtronic people helped save their lives.

How do those employees think of their work? Certainly not as just a matter of assembling parts. They keep in mind the big picture: it's all about saving lives, about allowing heart patients a better future. That sense of purpose is a great motivator!

But what about if you can't build motivation through a sense of purpose? After all, some jobs are far from life-saving. What can you do to keep your employees interested in their jobs?

Mary Kay keeps employees through inspiration and praise. The late Mary Kay Ash once said, "There are two things people want more than sex and money—recognition and praise." Women and men alike love working for this company. Ash, who founded the cosmetics giant in 1963, remained a personal inspiration to all of her employees for decades by praising high-achievers personally and sending them handwritten notes commending and thanking them.

According to Ash, one reason employees wanted to stay and work harder is because she takes the time to write two or three sentences on a piece of paper. In addition, the company sends out almost a half-million birthday, holiday, and anniversary cards every year. Can such cards actually affect the motivation of the Mary Kay sales force? Mary Kay thinks they do, and in the Mary Kay culture, they work. Of course, Mary Kay provides some nice material incentives as well, including pink Cadillacs, pearl necklaces, and diamond jewelry for the highest performers.

Maybe you don't produce life-saving medical devices. Maybe you can't offer your employees Cadillacs. But you certainly won't break the bank by giving out a few greeting cards or thank-you notes from time to time. It's also easy enough for you to remind your employees about the effects of their work on others, within your organization or in the community, the country, and the world.

It takes more than top salaries to keep good employees from leaving. Top performers want to work in a pleasant and progressive environment where they feel valued as people as much as skilled professionals.

How can you improve the environment in your particular part of the organization? There are many possibilities. Order pizzas for your employees to celebrate a significant event—or for no reason at all. Organize a group to work on some community project—such as painting a house, visiting a nursing home, or ringing bells for the Salvation Army. And make sure everyone knows this is a voluntary activity. When done in the right spirit, it reinforces the connection between the organization and the employee. It says, "We're all in this together, to help others." You can probably come up with dozens of other ideas.

Many companies, like Red Hat, the open source software company, have been known to provide incentives like a break room fully stocked with free snacks, group sporting event outings, and even beverages delivered during certain work days. Not only do these practices keep employees together during their "off" time, but they also serve to bond employees over positive activities. In the Gallup study referenced in Chapter 2, we also learned that having a friend at work can be crucial for employee engagement. What better way to foster the development of friendships than to encourage activities that go beyond the tasks at hand?

Step 3. Give Employees Honest Feedback, Praise, and Encouragement

One of the best things you can do for your employees is give them accurate and honest feedback. You may find, however, that this is one of the most difficult communication skills to master—especially when it involves giving negative feedback.

Most of us don't naturally accept negative comments very well. You may be familiar with that line by Groucho Marx: "People say I don't take criticism very well. But I say, what the hell do they know?" We laugh—but we realize that this is how we too tend to react. We feel uncomfortable, even offended. We might even get defensive, and then fume about the criticism and the person who criticized us.

Since we tend to take criticism badly, we usually like to avoid putting anyone else in the position of taking criticism. But providing honest feedback to employees is a major responsibility for you—one you'll assume more readily and with less discomfort if you appreciate the potential benefits and develop ways to make the best of a difficult situation.

A woman named Susan recalls an incident from years ago when her boss was brutally honest with her. It was an awful situation that turned into an opportunity for Susan to grow. Susan was just out of college at the time, working in her first job at a pharmaceutical company. After a meeting with several department managers, Susan's supervisor called Susan aside to give her some immediate feedback on how Susan had conducted herself in the meeting. It was a very difficult moment for Susan.

The supervisor told Susan that she'd been arrogant and a terrible listener in the meeting. She warned Susan that such behavior could be career suicide if it happened again. Later that day, Susan and her supervisor met to evaluate specifically what had taken place in the meeting and the impact it had. They also discussed how Susan could have behaved differently.

ROCKS AND CROCS

"It's all about rocks and crocs." That's what the manager told Bob shortly after hiring him. A few hours before his first divisional meeting, the manager briefed Bob on what to expect. She told Bob not to worry, but she felt he'd be better prepared to enter those unfamiliar waters if he knew where he could step safely and where the dangers lurked—the stepping-stones and the crocodiles, the "rocks and crocs."

Her briefing was a good lesson in company politics—and effective management. It's important to provide feedback, but it's also important to counsel your employees in advance, so that they're less likely to need a lot of feedback.

Despite her initial shock, Susan quickly realized the value of knowing the truth, and she wanted to thank her supervisor for possibly saving her career. In fact, she later asked the supervisor to be her mentor. The supervisor agreed to help that young, inexperienced, pushy, and somewhat arrogant new hire—and Susan is now a senior VP for the company.

The moral of this story? Honest feedback is a gift you can give your employees. It can change lives and help employees grow and develop. But how you package and deliver this gift will determine its effect on and value to the recipient.

The direct, to-the-point approach Susan's supervisor took in providing feedback was effective in that specific circumstance, primarily because it was immediate and because Susan was determined to succeed in her career. In another circumstance, with another employee, the supervisor probably would have handled things at least a little differently.

You have to use your best judgment, based on the employee's behavior and what you know about the

> **PROVIDING FEEDBACK** **SMART**
>
> Use the following strategies when giving employees feedback: **MANAGING**
>
> 1. Be sensitive to the reactions of your employee.
> 2. Talk about what you've observed, without making assumptions about the thoughts or feelings behind the employee's behaviors.
> 3. Focus on problems, not on personal issues or preferences. Your employees should be trying to do their jobs better, not please you.

employee. No matter how you decide to handle any situation, tell your employees the truth as you see it, even though it might make both you and the employees uncomfortable for a time. The discomfort is a small investment that will help you avoid worse problems down the line. We all tend to put more into our work when we feel that we're doing the job right, so appropriate feedback can make employees more motivated.

Feedback Strengthens Your Employees

Giving someone constructive or corrective feedback doesn't mean making the person understand the *right way* to do things. Instead, provide feedback to strengthen your employees. Encourage and allow them to explore better alternatives on their own, but be there when they need help.

How to Give Feedback

Here are three tips for providing feedback effectively:

- Be honest and accurate. Tell it like it is. Discuss specific actions and cite particulars—where, when, how.
- Review and evaluate. Review the effects of the employee's **TOOLS** actions, both positive and negative. What was the impact? What did it cost? Was it worth it?
- Replay and redo. If the situation could be repeated, how might the employee handle it differently? What did the employee learn from the experience? How can you share this with others in the organization?

Feedback is most effective and causes the least damage when you first establish with employees an explicit understanding of just how feedback will be provided. When you ask employees how they would best like to receive both corrective and positive feedback, you establish a foundation that avoids surprises and minimizes discomfort.

To set up a feedback process in advance, ask each of your employees the following questions:

- How would you prefer to receive feedback from me?
- What specifically would you like to receive feedback on?
- How can I help you feel comfortable receiving this information?
- Is there a particular format you would like me to use when giving you this information?
- How can I best give you feedback as we go along?
- Since you seem busy all the time, how do you recommend I get this information to you?

When asked, most employees will say that they sincerely appreciate and welcome feedback that helps them improve. The issue, however, is not the feedback itself, but the environment in which the feedback takes place. As manager, it's your responsibility to help establish a safe and respectful environment for giving and receiving feedback of all kinds. Minimize their discomfort so your feedback can maximize their motivation.

Protect Employees' Dignity and Self-Respect

When it comes to dignity and self-respect, we can learn something from the Japanese culture and the concept of saving face. The Japanese place a great deal of value on protecting a person's dignity and honoring his or her self-respect—helping a person avoid embarrassment at all costs. Of course, most Americans are less concerned about saving face, but dignity and self-respect are still important. Your employees

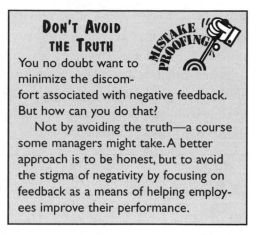

DON'T AVOID THE TRUTH

You no doubt want to minimize the discomfort associated with negative feedback. But how can you do that?

Not by avoiding the truth—a course some managers might take. A better approach is to be honest, but to avoid the stigma of negativity by focusing on feedback as a means of helping employees improve their performance.

don't want you to embarrass them with criticism. Be sensitive to their feelings while you help them learn how to avoid such mistakes in the future.

Here are some tips for creating an environment where you and your employees show respect for one another:

- Never criticize an employee in front of others. Offer corrective feedback only in private.
- Following corrective feedback, express optimism for the future and voice your appreciation for the employee's cooperation and efforts.
- Never point your finger at a person. It's a demeaning gesture and unprofessional.
- Thank an employee who retreats from a strongly held position. Let him or her know that you appreciate it.
- Never use a condescending tone of voice.
- Remember the Golden Rule. If you expect others to respect your sense of dignity, you should show them the same respect.
- Focus on improvement.

By using some of these strategies, you'll build a trusting and safe environment where employees welcome and appreciate your feedback and input—good or bad.

Praise and Encourage Employees to Success

In Chapter 2, I quoted William James, who said, "The deepest principle of human nature is the desire to be appreciated." This certainly rings true when it comes to the importance of praising and encouraging your employees. No matter what the industry or business, employees tend to push a little harder when you pat them on the back.

Unfortunately, the words "manager," "boss," and "supervisor" have all too often been synonymous with "criticism" and "pressure." Don't be miserly with your praise. Let people know when you're pleased—even if things aren't perfect. But be sincere.

ADJECTIVES OF PRAISE

If you're not very good at giving positive feedback, you may need to develop your vocabulary. Managers tend to overuse words like "nice," "good," and "great." Here are a few adjectives that you can use to praise more appropriately:

TOOLS

Thorough	Thoughtful
Complete	Imaginative
Innovative	Conscientious
Professional	Creative
Powerful	Admirable

Real Praise Isn't Phony Flattery

Don't start praising and encouraging your employees simply because this book suggests that you do so. Employees are savvy about "positive strokes" cloaked in false praise. Compliments that they perceive as being insincere or exaggerated or inappropriate will seem manipulative. The value of positive feedback is far greater when the praise is genuinely deserved and warranted.

Natural praise isn't forced or exaggerated. It isn't flattery. Don't try to motivate people by giving them more praise than their efforts are worth. Employees can see right through an insincere compliment for what it really is—manipulation. Praise and compliment from your heart. Say what you feel.

The Benefits of Praise

What are the benefits of praising your employees? Consider the following:

- You create trust.
- You encourage cooperation.
- You place the focus on improvement.

- You create possibilities.
- You clarify what it means to do a job well.
- You inspire employees to develop new skills.
- You build self-confidence in your employees.

We could sum up all of these benefits of praise in a single word—motivation.

Dos and Don'ts of Praising and Encouraging Employees

Praising and encouraging employees isn't always as easy and natural as you might expect. The following list of dos and don'ts will help you do it more effectively:

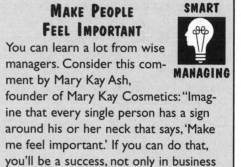

MAKE PEOPLE FEEL IMPORTANT

SMART MANAGING

You can learn a lot from wise managers. Consider this comment by Mary Kay Ash, founder of Mary Kay Cosmetics: "Imagine that every single person has a sign around his or her neck that says, 'Make me feel important.' If you can do that, you'll be a success, not only in business but in life as well."

- Don't negate your praise. For example, after a compliment, don't add, "It's about time."
- Do praise the deed, not the doer. Let people be pumped up by their work, not by you.
- Do praise people in public.
- Don't leave out any deserving employees when you praise.
- Do initiate an employee-of-the-month program and a team-of-the-month program.
- Do anticipate your team's successful outcomes and exceptional efforts. Plan in advance to celebrate successes and praise the people who made those successes happen.

Step 4. Build Employees' Confidence

It's important for you to treat your employees in ways that bolster their self-confidence. When your employees feel confident, they're more motivated and they can achieve more.

Why? Because when you show that you believe in people, you create expectations, and people tend to do what they're expected to do. Helping

> **CAUTION**
>
> ### Avoid the Big "But ..."
> One manager was very sensitive about providing negative feedback. So, whenever she had to correct an employee, she always started out with a few words of praise—a spoonful of sugar to help the medicine go down.
> There was a disadvantage to this strategy, however. After a while, she couldn't just compliment any of her employees. Whenever she said something nice, the employee would tense up and wait for the inevitable "But ..." that signaled the start of a criticism. She had to work hard to regain her employees' trust, so they could accept praise from her without being suspicious that it was just a spoonful of sugar.

others feel motivated means having high expectations about what they can accomplish. By showing this kind of faith in your employees, you bolster their self-confidence.

Think of a time when you felt extraordinarily self-confident about something. Remember how it made you feel? Almost super-human, right? Chances are, whatever it was you felt confident about, you were able to perform with greater ease and overall success. And you were no doubt very motivated about it from the start.

Research confirms that men and women who have high self-esteem and confidence—regardless of their age, background, or education—feel unique, special, competent, empowered, secure, and connected to those around them. Now isn't that the way you want your employees to feel?

Here are a few ways to help build your employees' self-esteem and confidence:

■ Seek their opinions and suggestions and then put them to use.
■ Encourage your employees to be positive about each other. Don't allow an employee to dismiss his or her success. Document and discuss achievements together.
■ Help your employees set ambitious goals, then help them work toward those goals.
■ Let your employees know whenever someone else compliments them.

Remember: confident employees are motivated employees.

What Goes Around Comes Around

When you influence the self-confidence of your employees, it can be a reciprocal process: they can influence the confidence you feel about yourself. That's a nice bonus for just doing your job as their manager.

If employees tell you just how good they believe you can be as their manager, you may quickly find yourself adjusting your self-concept and self-expectations to be congruent with what your employees perceive. And, yes, you'll feel more motivated as well.

Here are some ways you can improve your own self-confidence:

- Never tolerate mediocrity. Draw upon any spiritual beliefs you may have.
- Improve yourself by helping others improve their lives and achieve their goals. You never learn as much as when you help others to learn. Examine the differences you've made in the lives of others in recent months.
- When others tell you how valuable you are, believe them. Don't shrug off or downplay praise.

Even a confident manager can sometimes experience a drop in self-confidence. Be aware of it when it happens. And remember that low self-esteem and low self-confidence can undermine your motivation and seriously hinder your ability to achieve your full potential and lead others to achieving theirs. In the words of John Peers, "You can't lead a cavalry charge if you think you look funny on a horse."

Motivating Employees Beyond Fear

We've all experienced that gut-twisting, panicked feeling when an unexpected force of change or loss grips our souls and drenches our palms with a cold sweat. Some freeze like a fawn in floodlights, and others are at their best when living with two dollars to their name, in the middle of a blizzard—amidst fireworks and an attack by a pack of wild hyenas (or some such unlikely stream of events).

Whether you operate best when your *amygdala* is on overload and kicking you into fight or flight mode or not, it's important to recognize the effect that fear can have on you and your employees. Otherwise, your team may end up paralyzed—or, worse yet, fleeing for greener hills.

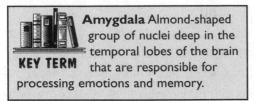

Amygdala Almond-shaped group of nuclei deep in the temporal lobes of the brain **KEY TERM** that are responsible for processing emotions and memory.

If instead you can help your employees overcome fear, you will build their trust in your management skills, and in the security of your organization. You will gain their loyalty and commitment to hard work, knowing that it will bring relief.

Few knew fear as severe as that experienced by corporate speaker Jeanette Towne, who is also CEO of a high-tech firm and author of *From Prisoner to President*. Towne was once trapped as the victim of heinous domestic abuse at the hands of her then-husband. After having a hammer literally held to her head, she escaped, and went on to become president of her own company. The process of enduring unfathomable abuse, while simultaneously pursuing unprecedented career success, taught her a few things about fear and management.

"Arriving at the doorstep of death with blood running down my face more than once, with the perpetrator being the person who was supposed to protect me, I learned how to *not* freeze amidst chaos and fear—but to keep my cool, keep breathing, and keep moving," states Towne. "I also learned how to invest in myself and stay on course with my goals and dreams, even when those in my environment wanted me to give up. These are the same principles I use in management to this day—to keep my employees motivated and safe during times of change or uncertainty."

Here are three tips she used to survive fear, which she recommends for managers wishing to motivate their employees and build trust:

1. Detach from the Drama. Nothing in business is a life-or-death situation. Detach from fear before coming up with a reactive plan. Detach from the worst-case scenario before communicating a fear-based message. So you're losing your biggest client? That is devastating news. But before delivering the news over the loud speaker, get over your own fear that "this means our company is going to end, and we are going to all live on the street." Process, think, breathe, and come up with logical (rather than emotional) explanations and solutions—or at least concise and productive challenges to solve—before projecting fear onto your employees. Answer questions from your employees with as much calm as you can— remaining honest but open to potential opportunities and the bigger picture.

2. Focus on What Isn't Scary. Even when Towne was in an abusive relationship, she took time to educate herself—

DON'T FEED FEAR SMART

"I have often been afraid, but I would not give in to it. I made myself act as though I was not afraid and gradually my fear disappeared."

MANAGING

—Theodore Roosevelt

Fear is like a wolf that, if fed, will devour you. Instead, walk ahead confidently towards a better tomorrow. Trust that there is a solution, even if you don't see it yet.

secretly taking classes to better herself, accepting help. Focusing on the positive outcomes and opportunities amidst change or chaos allows your employees to keep moving during seemingly blinding storms. Would you rather stare at a dead tree blocking the trail or hike around it in search of new signs of life? Help employees come up with strategies to keep themselves moving ahead toward productive ends. Help them prepare for change while alternate routes still exist, and prepare yourself similarly.

3. Cut Out the Toxins. If an employee or situation is causing abuse to others in the group, and this is the source of the fear, you may need to take action. Don't be afraid to remove the toxins so the rest of the organization can thrive. If the fear is based on a real threat, deal with the threat. Don't be an ostrich or Pollyanna and think it's all going to get better by ignoring it. Be courageous, and take proactive leaps. Your strength to make tough decisions will instill trust from your employees.

De-Motivators? What De-Motivators?

There are many factors that can weaken your employees' motivation to perform well. The point of this chapter has been, however, to give you ideas for overcoming those factors—and for not contributing to the list of factors.

You want to maximize the potential for positive motivation by hiring people who seem naturally more intrinsically motivated and should be less affected by de-motivating factors—and less likely to become de-motivating factors themselves. You then want to work at keeping your motivated employees on the job and performing at their best. That means praising them when they do well, of course. But it also means knowing how to provide corrective feedback—and having the courage and sensitivity to do the job.

You can't avoid negative factors. That's life. But the care and concern you show in reacting to them will help your employees overcome those factors and become even more motivated.

Manager's Checklist for Chapter 8

☑ Take responsibility for minimizing the de-motivating effects of workplace influences on your employees. You can directly or indirectly impact employees' self-esteem, their motivation, their long-term interests, and their overall ability to love what they do for a living.

☑ Performance reviews can be a valuable source of corrective and positive feedback and an effective way to measure a person's progress against established criteria and outcomes. But they can also be devastating if you use them simply to rate an employee, to objectify an individual.

☑ Always keep the "attitude vultures" at bay.

☑ Motivate employees beyond their own personal fears.

☑ You can fight against de-motivational factors if you hire the best people, retain them, give them honest feedback and encouragement, and build their confidence.

☑ Research confirms that men and women with high self-esteem and confidence feel motivated, competent, empowered, secure, and connected to those around them.

Clear the Path to Employee Performance

Use Motivation to Impact the Whole System

The motivation challenge for managers goes beyond individuals to a larger context. Factors above and beyond your immediate work area have a substantial impact on the motivation of your employees (in many cases, even more impact than any specific efforts you might make to positively influence motivation). Dealing with this larger context or situation is often referred to as thinking in terms of the "whole system," or just "system" for short.

You were encouraged in Chapter 1 to ask yourself a question: "Am I positively or negatively influencing my employees' motivation?" We've looked at ways to emphasize positive influences and minimize negative influences that affect your employees' motivation.

My focus in this book has generally been on what happens within your work unit and on what you can control in your environment.

Now I am going beyond that environment, to get you to consider the system and the influence of its forces and patterns. The system generally has a tremendous effect on the motivation of your employees, often indirectly and subtly. That's how it works in systems—everything that happens affects everything else.

Thinking in Terms of the System

You have to be attentive to how all the parts of your system are operating together and influencing each other. If you can do this, you can better manage the effects of those influences on your employees. With a systems perspective, you begin to recognize that any single action can cause ripples throughout the organization. A little negativity or lack of thought in dealing with one employee can quickly affect the quality of your relationships with other employees and their levels of motivation and commitment to their jobs.

KEY TERM **System** Unified, multi-dimensional forces and patterns found in natural, created, and human environments. There are always four types of elements in a system: inputs, processes, outputs, and feedback.

All organizations are systems, and likewise, your particular unit is a system within a larger system. In any system, the behavior of each element affects the behavior of the system as a whole, which in turn affects each element. Systems thinking has broad implications for how you manage your employees and what you can and should do to influence their motivation.

Big Consequences of a Small Decision

Jim is the manager of a car wash, one of a dozen in a chain. Business is booming, and his employees are motivated to do a great job, to take pride in their work. Life is good.

One morning, the corporate marketing director decides to save some money and not print promotional fliers on the better-quality, heavier-stock paper the company has been using for years. She goes to a cheaper paper, figuring, "What's the big deal? The flier still serves the same purpose—telling the customer about our car washes and other services."

That's it. From her perspective, it's a simple business decision.

But that decision is not so simple in the context of the whole business system. When the fliers arrive, Jim's employees notice that they look a little cheaper, less professional. They joke about "the new company look." But then they figure, if the company is getting more relaxed about the appearance of its promotional materials, maybe they can get more relaxed, too. They start dressing more casually, some even looking a little sloppy. Before long, they're no longer giving customers the same quality of go-the-extra-mile service.

Then Jim's detailing specialist decides that, since everyone else seems more casual, a little less particular about what they're doing, he can take a little less care in how he details the customers' cars. What's the big deal, right?

Soon Jim's customers are noticing a difference in the overall atmosphere of the car wash, and some of them decide that maybe they don't need to come in quite as often. And when new customers come around, their first impression isn't good enough to make them want to come back. They probably don't recommend Jim's car wash place to their friends either.

Now Jim's got a problem. His car wash is going downhill. That's bad (especially when the company execs review the quarterly figures). He can't quite figure out why business has gotten worse. But now he's got to do something—fast—to bring in more business. Maybe he can offer some added services, but the workers aren't going to like that—especially after adopting their more relaxed approach to service. Now Jim's got financial problems and morale problems—and things are only getting worse.

If Jim were to think about his car wash in terms of the whole business system, he'd understand better what was happening—and he'd have some on-target ideas about how to restore his business. In fact, Jim probably would have anticipated the effects of that marketing decision on the motivation of his employees. He would have discussed the decision with his employees and explained how it was a way to cut costs, but that it didn't reflect any change in attitude about the importance of appearances and great service. He'd certainly be more attentive to any element in the company system that might affect his particular car wash—so he'd be a more effective manager.

That's how systems thinking works. Systems thinking might have helped Jim avoid the serious problems he now faces.

Think about your own situation. You can probably remember several instances when actions had unforeseen consequences. Maybe those actions affected operations in an adjacent work area or upset employees in a faraway branch of the organization. That's how any action can cause ripple effects throughout an entire system.

If you understand that a business is a complex social and mechanical system, with dynamic connections among forces and patterns, you can work on making that system better, more effective, and more efficient—in both your immediate area and beyond. And in the process, you can positively influence your employees' motivation and work to minimize or alleviate the de-motivators within the system.

The Human Side of Operations

This chapter began by defining a system as "unified, multi-dimensional forces and patterns." For a business, the system involves organizational structures, communication channels, management policies, administrative procedures, and so on. People work in this system and are potentially its most important element. Business systems are largely controlled by human nature and by the work of dozens, hundreds, or even thousands of people, all connected in various ways.

You cannot overestimate the importance of the human side of operations. Now more than ever, people are critical to every business system. In fact, the "social side" of operations can be as vital as all of the structures, channels, policies, procedures, and whatever else. No matter what machinery and computers and other equipment your organization may have, the relationships and the communication among your people are what determine from the start whether the organization will be a success.

US VERSUS THEM

CAUTION

When you discuss with your employees the people and actions outside your work unit, be very careful. Don't get into Us versus Them.

It's easy to slip into questioning and criticizing the decisions and actions of other managers and departments, especially when you disagree with them and you're upset about the effects on your employees. But it's a bad way to manage. It gives off the message that you don't respect people in other parts of the organization, and it says it's OK for employees to feel that way as well. It can only lead to further disagreements and frustrations. What you want is to build mutually supportive relationships with other work groups so you can work together to solve problems.

Look at the prevalence of social media like Facebook, Twitter, and LinkedIn, and you will infer that not only are social networks vital to logistical operations, but they are also a vehicle from which people derive personal and professional value. Even in leisure time, many people spend time browsing profiles of their friends and colleagues and finding new ways to connect. If you can harness this social power and use it to optimize your systems and infuse cohesiveness among team members, you will increase your odds of functioning as a highly-performing unit.

So much depends on the connections among the people in your organization. But time and time again, managers underestimate the impact that social interaction has on the system. The truth is that, without people, business systems don't work.

Studies of human behavior and productivity show consistently that when you cut out or ignore the social part of work, motivation, productivity, and efficiency drop. Social interaction is not only the glue of the human network, but also a force that motivates all of us and stimulates us to be productive and efficient.

"The Buzz" Keeps Us Learning and Productive

At a busy air traffic control center, workers were asked to wear devices that would cover their ears and suppress the noise in the tower. Management wanted to increase the efficiency and productivity of the air traffic controllers.

The result? No increase at all. In fact, a big drop in productivity.

Managers later learned that the workers had been accustomed to subconsciously picking up on all of the conversations taking place around them as they worked, so that they were continuously learning things from their environment. When the devices shut them off from the *buzz* of people interacting, they became impaired and less effective in their jobs. This is just one example of the importance of social interaction—even subconscious social interaction—in a business system. If you think about it for a moment, you can probably remember times when

---

NEVER LOSE TOUCH

SMART

MANAGING

Do you remember the poem by Rudyard Kipling, "If"? We probably all read it in school, and maybe memorized it, before forgetting it as we grew older. That's a shame, because now is when it could be most useful to us.

One line from the poem is particularly important for managers because it's a reminder that you should be able "to walk with kings" but not lose "the common touch." In other words, you should feel comfortable working with other managers and the leaders of the organization, but never lose touch with your employees and with their perceptions and their feelings.

someone in your organization forgot about the importance of people—and learned a similar lesson the hard way.

Stop Workplace Drama

You may be amazed by how drama can hijack your team's emotions, energy, and efforts before you bank on the island of success. You might not even realize drama exists until your star performer is so drained she quits, or your customers complain to you that your workplace is riddled with negative service and bad attitudes. By then, the boat has sprung leaks, and you are sinking to the bottom of the lake.

Drama, as defined by Marlene Chism, speaker and author of *Stop Workplace Drama* , is "any obstacle to your peace or prosperity." Among your employees, drama may manifest itself as gossip, backstabbing, power struggles, making excuses for why something can't be done, remaining stuck in the past, or being unwilling to accept even positive change. None of these forms of drama do anything except keep your organization stuck in the muck.

The Person with Clarity Navigates the Ship

All drama, Chism feels, has similar elements, and by cutting through the fog and getting clear, you and your employees will stop beating each other with the oars, and start working collectively. It is then that the real magic and progress occurs. As Chism states, "The one with clarity navigates the ship. Everyone else shovels coal in the boiler room." For the purpose of getting clear as a manager and passing that clarity on to employees, Chism has developed a clever and powerful eight-step "Stop Your Drama Methodology." Her empower-

SMART

MANAGING

ISLAND LANGUAGE

The island language is something that Chism recommends in order to "lighten up" the Stop Workplace Drama discussion. Here are some key terms:

- *The island*: The place of paradise or success you want to arrive.
- *The gap:* The sometimes overwhelming distance you have to travel to get there.
- *The fog:* The lack of clarity that often occurs in the gap, temporarily causing you to feel blind.

ment techniques involve cutting through the fog of drama that would keep your team from its goals, motivating and equipping employees to row together toward "the island" of success, and inspiring them to arrive as a team and celebrate. This is essentially clearing the path for your employees.

The first step in Chism's methodology involves getting clear. Why is it that managers often skip this phase or struggle to retain it? It could be because they're bombarded with distractions—from sales goals, to customer complaints, to the economy, to the weather—making it easy to get sidetracked before even launching their boat. Chism states in her book, "Excuses always inhibit growth ... But guess what—you have to make the decision first. Then the time, resources, and people will appear and help you get to the island."

Even after getting clear, you will experience a "gap" between where you are, and where you want to be. To navigate the gap, you must "clear the fog." This means eliminating the obstacles or lack of clarity that will keep you stuck muddling around in dodgy sea currents. Sometimes, it can take a while to uncover everything inside the fog, but

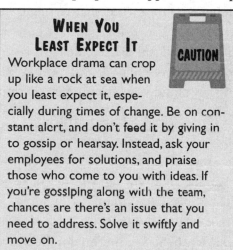

WHEN YOU LEAST EXPECT IT **CAUTION**
Workplace drama can crop up like a rock at sea when you least expect it, especially during times of change. Be on constant alert, and don't feed it by giving in to gossip or hearsay. Instead, ask your employees for solutions, and praise those who come to you with ideas. If you're gossiping along with the team, chances are there's an issue that you need to address. Solve it swiftly and move on.

once you do, you have choices and action steps to take. Be honest with yourself and others as you strive to get clear. Maybe you need more staff members or a readjustment of your budget allocation. Maybe you need more regular meetings. Maybe you need purple widgets. Whatever it is, if you're clear, you'll keep moving—because you know where you're headed and what you need to get there. If you assess what you need up front and along the way, and stay true to that vision even when storm clouds appear out of nowhere, you'll remain well-equipped to proceed.

As a means of remaining clear, Chism advocates providing a strategy in the form of policies and procedures, and then communicating often and effectively—asking for regular weekly feedback from employees on how the journey is going and what can be improved. If you don't ask, how can you expect employees to remain dedicated and committed to the course? Such procedures keep the fog at bay.

What if you still experience employee complaints or drama along the way? Tell your employees that you expect them to come to you with ideas for solutions, along with any complaints or problems. Give them five minutes to air a grievance, and then ask for an idea to solve it. This will not only give them the opportunity to be stars in your organization but will also get their minds beyond the drama of the problem, and into the harmony of finding a solution. Think of it like handing a paddle to the employee sitting in the boat and asking, "Now what would you suggest doing with this?" The answer might be a no-brainer. And if it is, then you've eliminated the need for employees to waste energy with complaining and empowered them instead with a can-do attitude. Even if the ideas they present don't work, you're instilling in them a value of searching for solutions, which is bound to ripple through the group.

Celebrate—It's Motivational

Finally, one of the most important steps in stopping workplace drama involves celebrating success when you succeed. Chism likens this to claiming victory when you reach the island, and taking a little time to relax. This is important for building morale in the team and fostering trust in your leadership. It also gives them a rewarding and useful recharge before setting out for the next destination. If your destination is far away, set up smaller milestones you can celebrate—and do it with gusto—to motivate them along the way. And remember, keep the team clear about the destination, so they don't get distracted by a closer island that may appear more tempting but without the greater reward. Finally, have fun!

Developing Insight into Your Business System

If you want to develop further insight into your organization's business system, and consider how those forces and patterns might be influencing the motivation of your people, start by answering some of the following questions:

STEPS TO STOPPING WORKPLACE DRAMA

Chism's 8-part Stop Your Drama Methodology as defined in her book, *Stop Workplace Drama*, includes the following steps:

1. **Clear the Fog:** Eliminate obstacles and existing drama so you can get clear on what you want to achieve.

TOOLS

2. **Identify the Gap:** Determine what ground you have to cover to meet your goals.
3. **Tell Yourself the Truth:** Be honest about changes that need to occur, either in yourself, or in your organization.
4. **Reinvent and Realign:** Adjust based on what you are learning in the process.
5. **Stop Relationship Drama:** Make the relationships in your life healthy, including your relationship with yourself, your job, etc.
6. **Master Your Energy:** Stay healthy in mind and body—and proactive instead of reactive.
7. **Release Resistance:** Let go of the things you resist—and ask for help seeing these things.
8. **Become a Creator:** Build your legacy and push your imagination to see the potential.

- What is the current business situation in your marketplace? Is it positive or negative? Are people optimistic or pessimistic?
- How do your employees feel about the leaders?
- What values are practiced (not just preached) in your organization?
- What strategies are you implementing in the market?
- What impact is management having on the atmosphere and culture of the organization?
- What are the important processes in your organization? How is your organization structured? Is this structure based on functions, on markets, or on geography?
- How do organizational policies directly support or hinder the work of employees?
- Are employees' roles engaging, challenging, enriching, and fulfilling?
- Are work tasks well-designed, appropriately staffed, and supported?
- Are employees well-qualified for the work they do?
- Do employees and managers work together to achieve results?

Questions like these will help you think about the interdependencies and interconnections among people, functions, strategies, and organizational success. They will help you consider how your system is set up and identify areas for improvement. If you come up with ambiguous answers, it means that the system is operating inefficiently, that people do not clearly understand their roles, and that people may be working at cross purposes with one another and will experience frustrations that will negatively affect their motivation.

Once you've gained some insight into your organization's system and its direct and indirect influences on people and their motivation, what do you do with what you've learned? More specifically, how can you use this insight in your efforts to improve employees' motivation? Here are a few suggestions:

- If your employees aren't performing up to expectations, don't assume that the problem is with them—or with you. The problem is likely the result of something in the system. (What can you do? I'll get to that later in this chapter.)
- As you consider specific ways to improve the motivation of your employees, think about the possible effects on the rest of the system. Review your ideas with employees before implementing them. Don't be territorial. (This, too, is something I'll discuss a little later.)
- If you know that something in the system is affecting your employees, don't be complacent about it—even if you feel your employees are adapting well. Things may be OK—or they may seem that way. It may be time to act, to save your employees. (I'll get into this question right away.)

SYSTEMS AND MOTIVATION

SMART MANAGING

Think systems when you think motivation. Employees who have to continually adapt to systems that don't support their work ultimately resign themselves to several perceptions:

- "Management cares more about making the rules than about performance."
- "Management doesn't understand what's going on."
- "Management will never let us do what we really need to do."
- "Management says one thing, but does another."

Any of these perceptions will definitely undermine motivation.

Adapting to the System

You no doubt appreciate employees who can adapt to situations, who can adjust to the system. But you may not realize the cost of that adapting and adjusting.

> **Restraining forces** Factors that impede performance. Sometimes you can do something to minimize or eliminate restraining forces. But within whole business systems, these forces may be driving one process while restraining another. If that's the case, then you can only try to lessen the negative effects on employee performance and motivation.
>
> **KEY TERM**

When employees are continually adapting to systems that don't support their efforts—because of structures, policies, or procedures—what happens? They usually respond in one of three ways:

- They fight the system.
- They accept the situation.
- They withdraw.

Having to adapt to *restraining forces* in a system is frustrating and stressful for most people. Employees all have different capacities for adapting—and you'll quickly see that in the effects on their motivation and performance.

Of course, you can't simply do away with any structures, policies, and procedures that act as restraining forces. They're probably in place for good reasons. On the other hand, don't assume that they're all necessary and good. Sometimes a structure, policy, or procedure is obsolete or is a good idea in theory but simply doesn't work in practice. If that's the case, then you should work to change it or get rid of it.

You need to think in terms of the whole system. No matter how simple a particular situation or activity may seem, consider its possible and probable effects on your organization's work design, culture, management, and other factors.

Changing the System

So far this chapter has focused on the effects of the system on employees' motivation. You've gotten some advice on how you can identify the influences of patterns and forces in the system and work to maximize the good effects and minimize the bad ones.

But it may not be enough to react to the effects of the system. Sometimes you've got to try to *change* the system. If you find that employees' motivation is being undermined by the system, one of your options is to act to remove or reduce the restraining forces of the system. To be more precise, if you're a smart manager who understands the psychology of motivation, you encourage and help your employees to act themselves. To do that, use the following approach:

1. Invite your employees to meet with you to discuss the situation.
2. Let them tell you their perceptions and feelings. What problem(s) have they perceived? Sure, you may know it all already, but they need to be involved from the start. Besides, what if you've missed or misinterpreted something?
3. Ask them to suggest ways to improve the situation. Welcome any and all suggestions, no matter how unrealistic they may appear, for two reasons. One, you want to encourage open thinking, so you're not reacting to a problem but thinking in terms of the big picture. Two, if the problem requires action, it's probably already caused a lot of negative feelings—and a forum can help everybody express those feelings and vent.
4. Decide together on the best solution. Seek *consensus* in doing this. "Best" here may mean easiest or most practical or ideal, depending on your situation. Or it may mean several solutions.

> **KEY TERM**
>
> **Consensus** This is different from "majority rules." A consensus decision is one that everyone can agree to and that everyone has a chance to help shape in one way or another. When there is a consensus, everyone feels a commitment to the course of action decided on.

5. Determine who will take charge of the solution. Don't volunteer: let your employees decide. If they want you to take charge, you should accept only if you don't empower one or more of them to do so. But you should also involve a few of them: this is a shared action, a collaborative project.
6. Set a schedule. Who will be doing what, and by when? An action plan without a timeline is often just a plan for inaction.

> ### FACILITATE, DON'T RUN
> Don't run the "changing the system" meeting that you have
> with your employees. Just facilitate it; help your employees take
> the basic steps themselves.
>   Focus on the process, not the product. Maybe you won't be
> able to come up with any practical ideas for improving the situation. Or
> maybe you'll try something but it won't work. At least your employees will
> be better because of the way you've all worked together. And that's a sig-
> nificant benefit in itself. Treat the failure as a learning experience, so your
> employees will grow in their empowerment.

7. Schedule a meeting to evaluate the effects of the action. Again, this
   should be up to your employees. When do they believe that it would
   be best to assess the situation again?

Don't end your meeting before you've covered this agenda. Otherwise, the problem will simply linger. If employees understand that there's
a process to attack problems and that they're directly involved in defining
the problem and its solution, they'll feel motivated to take part and to fulfill the commitments they made in the meeting.

Continue Being Proactive

What will you accomplish through this meeting with your employees on
changing the system? That depends on the follow-up meeting, you say.

Well, yes and no. You've already taken steps to improve motivation,
because you've given your employees the responsibility and authority to
do something about their situation. This action alone may bring about
some positive changes, which would be great. But even if not much
changes over the short run, just working together like this can improve
employee motivation, which will ultimately result in positive changes.

Whatever the case, don't stop with what you've done. After your
employees have evaluated the situation, propose forming a team to mon-
itor the work environment. That way, maybe you can anticipate restraining forces and other negative influences in the system *before* they
seriously damage employee motivation and morale.

Caring for the System

You now know that when you're considering ways to improve the motivation of your employees, you need to think about how the changes you make might affect the rest of the system. Maybe you believe that you've got the right, and even the responsibility, to make *any* changes for the good of your employees. Or maybe you believe that whatever changes you make will have little or no effect outside your area. Be careful. It's risky to make changes in your area without considering their impact on other areas in the system.

Achieving any business objective requires the alignment of many system forces—people, structures, procedures, policies. Of course, it's rarely as simple as it may sound. Often, unavoidably, other forces get in the way.

A system element may be both a driving force and a restraining force, depending on your perspective. Unfortunately, sometimes managers and employees get too focused on their particular perspective. The result? They become territorial. Sometimes this means disputes over resources. Sometimes it means all-out turf wars. Either way, each group is trying to optimize its own part of the organization. But ironically, the groups always end up *suboptimizing* the whole system.

KEY TERM **Suboptimize** When people promote parts of the organization without thinking in terms of the whole, the system can't develop to its potential. This result is the opposite of synergy—the whole becomes less than the sum of its parts.

Traditionally, managers have been expected to be strong—to fight for what they wanted and needed: resources, responsibilities, rewards, and respect. Upper management has often encouraged this territorial thinking by providing incentives to units that have met or surpassed their performance goals, and by expecting managers to solve problems on their own. These incentives have often led to unhealthy competition within the organization. Meanwhile, the solo approach to problems has often meant that solving a problem in one area causes problems to arise in other areas.

Smart managers now realize the importance of thinking and acting in terms of the greater good of the system, of balancing the various parts of the whole to achieve optimal results for the organization. But managers are, well, only human, so they don't always instinctively do what's best for the whole organization.

Employees Know Their Side of the Wall

One factor that keeps you from working in terms of the system might be your employees. That's right, because, in many organizations, employees are focused on what's expected of them, as individuals and as a group. They may not get the big picture. To put it simply, they know their side of the wall—and probably too little about what's on the other side. In that case, you may need to share your "system" perspective with them.

Let's look at an example, a fairly common situation. Your employees aren't meeting your performance expectations. So, being a good manager, you ask them why not. They tell you what they perceive to be getting in their way. Maybe it's a procedure that just complicates their lives. Or a form that they're required to complete, even though it makes no sense to them. Or a policy that prevents them from doing certain tasks more efficiently. They can identify the forces that are restraining them, but they don't know anything about the reasons for these forces. So they feel like they're pushing against a wall—or sometimes even banging their heads against it!

You feel caught.

You could do something to improve their situation for the short term. You might, for instance, allow them to cut corners in the procedure or ignore the form or disregard the policy. That may be good for their motivation, at least for a little while, but it's bad managing.

You could decide instead to educate your people on the reasons behind those restraining forces, to help them see themselves in the context of the whole system. Give them the big picture—with their wall in it. It may not be what they want to hear, but don't be surprised if they stay motivated to perform now that they understand. (And if you can't give them good reasons, maybe they can come up with ways to reduce or eliminate those forces.)

Challenge: Understand and Improve the System

This brings us back to the title of this chapter: "Clear the Path to Employee Performance." An organization is filled with obstacles. This is because in interdependent systems you can never get everything working just right. There will always be loose ends and mix-ups.

However, if you acknowledge this basic reality, learn as much about the system as possible, and make improving it an important goal, over time you'll reduce those obstacles. That's the big challenge for any manager—and an important part of your job. If you think in terms of the system, you'll help the organization run better and you'll positively influence the motivation of your employees.

Manager's Checklist for Chapter 9

☑ Think in terms of the "whole system." Every organization is a complex social and mechanical system, with dynamic connections among forces and patterns. Factors above and beyond your immediate work area substantially influence the motivation of your employees.

☑ Never underestimate the impact of social interaction on the business system.

☑ Managers appreciate employees who can adapt to the system. But there's a cost: employees who are continually adapting to systems will fight the systems, accept the situation, or withdraw. Adapting is stressful for most people—and you, as a manager, may pay the price in terms of the effects on employees' motivation and performance.

☑ If there are restraining forces undermining the motivation of your employees, consider working with your employees to change the system, to remove or reduce these forces.

☑ Don't suboptimize the system. Provide whatever resources, responsibilities, rewards, and respect your employees need to do their jobs better, but from a systems perspective. Territorial attitudes hurt the organization, as actions to improve the situation in one area often make the situation worse in other areas.

☑ Harness the power of social media and use it to optimize your systems and infuse cohesiveness amongst your teams.

☑ Stop workplace drama in its tracks!

☑ Celebrate! It's motivational!

☑ Think and act in terms of the greater good of the system. That way, you and your employees will help the entire organization achieve optimal results.

Chapter 10

Inspiring Motivated Teamwork from the Head and the Heart

Let Teams Know They Make a Difference

n the world of business, we first learn about such matters as marketing strategy, production, and finance. We tend to neglect that organizations are about people and the relationships they develop to work together, the teamwork that makes individuals into a community and motivates them to do more. As Patrick Lencioni says in *The Five Dysfunctions of a Team*, "Not finance. Not strategy. Not technology. It's teamwork that remains the ultimate competitive advantage, because it is so powerful and so rare." This chapter focuses on the benefits of teamwork and what you can do to inspire and develop the motivational power of teams.

The Human Side of Teamwork

Trying to make a difference and having the opportunity to work closely with others to achieve a goal are two of the most powerful motivators for accomplishing challenging work. Put these two things together and you have the potential for a high-performing team.

When building teamwork within your organization, you have to be *motivated* and be *motivating*. Then, if you understand how people interrelate, you can inspire team spirit and increase the motivation that drives the members of your team.

> **TEAM DYSFUNCTIONS**
> **CAUTION**
> What can get in the way of smooth teamwork? In *The Five Dysfunctions of a Team*, Lencioni highlights the following:
> - Dysfunction 1: Absence of Trust
> - Dysfunction 2: Fear of Conflict
> - Dysfunction 3: Lack of Commitment
> - Dysfunction 4: Avoidance of Accountability
> - Dysfunction 5: Inattention to Results

Let's begin with the importance of showing your employees that you care about them. If you genuinely care about your employees and show them, you'll meet their basic need to be cared about. That feeling of assurance should help them find greater motivation to work harder and smarter.

Caring Makes a Difference

Showing that you care about people is not expensive; in fact, it doesn't cost the organization anything. It often requires only a minimum amount of energy. Yet it can greatly build up the assets of any company—human assets.

If you want to be a motivating manager, you have to show you care. What does that mean? Managers who care:

- Inspire their employees to work harder.
- Make their employees feel good about the work they're doing.
- Find out what their employees are really good at.
- Ask their employees what they'd like to do.
- Encourage a team to do more than all of its members could do as individuals.
- Work with their employees as colleagues, not over them as bosses.
- Excite their employees about doing things they never considered doing.
- Treat people consistently and fairly.
- Really listen to what their employees have to say.
- Build teamwork among workers and management.

In other words, a manager who cares about his or her employees inspires them to care about what they're doing—and they become more motivated to achieve.

Lead Them from the Heart

The word *encouragement* has as its root the Latin word *cor*, which means "heart." When you encourage employees, you actually give them heart. You're showing that you care about them. You lead them with feeling.

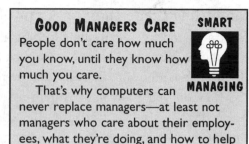

GOOD MANAGERS CARE

SMART MANAGING

People don't care how much you know, until they know how much you care.

That's why computers can never replace managers—at least not managers who care about their employees, what they're doing, and how to help them improve.

If that idea makes you a little uncomfortable, that's normal, considering the traditional attitudes and expectations of the business world. But consider the following story.

When Barbara Walters interviewed General Norman Schwarzkopf following the Gulf War, she asked him how he would most like to be remembered. His answer: *That he loved his family. That he loved his troops. And that they loved him.* This was probably not the answer millions of television viewers expected to hear that night.

Schwarzkopf had almost absolute power, as a general, to command his troops to do anything, even die. Yet he cared about those people serving under him—and he wanted them to know that he cared. That feeling motivated his soldiers to go above and beyond the call of duty.

You can't command your employees as Schwarzkopf commanded his soldiers. But if you care about them and show that you care, you encourage them, you give them heart. In a word, you help them find greater motivation in what they do.

THE IDEAL EPITAPH

TRICKS OF THE TRADE

What's the key to working well with people? It may be to live your ideal epitaph. In other words, carve an inscription into your future tombstone, then live to earn it.

How would you like to be remembered? General Norman Schwarzkopf answered that question simply: That he loved his family. That he loved his troops. And that they loved him.

Take a moment to think about how you'd like to be remembered. Write it out (in 25 words or so). Keep these words where you can read them regularly. Then, try to live up to your tombstone inscription.

Motivating Leadership: An Affair of the Heart

Motivating managers care about leading, they care about their employees, and they care about what their organizations do. That caring motivates them—and it motivates those around them. Does this sound like you?

How do you show your employees that you care about them? By respecting their individual dignity. Help them sustain and build that dignity through their work. How? By allowing them to think and to make choices, as was emphasized in earlier chapters. Allow them to be human. (Consider the comment by Anthony Eden: "Nothing is more destructive of human dignity than a rule which imposes a mute and blind obedience.")

Give employees support when they need it. When you ask your employees to go the extra mile or to step outside of their comfort zones, the care you show and the encouragement you provide will help them resist the debilitating effects of stress that they may be feeling.

You can also show that you care about people, through your leadership, in ways that reinforce a powerful message: "We are all in this together—we're a team."

How are you a leader? That's a key question. Addressing it properly would go far beyond the scope of this chapter. But the essential point this book has been making about motivation is just as valid for leadership: you influence and you lead more naturally and more effectively from within than from the outside.

What does that mean? Well, just as you motivate best when you help people find reasons to care and to strive, you lead best when you inspire people to follow your example and emulate you. The best leaders are those who work closely with their people, who are different from them, not by higher rank but by greater responsibility. The following words of wisdom from Jules Ormont merit yet another spot on the office wall of every manager: "A great leader never sets himself above his followers except in carrying responsibilities."

You Must Have Fire in Your Belly

To motivate your employees, you must be motivated yourself. This kind of managerial motivation comes from the fire in your belly, the desire to do something important, to make a difference in the world. It's this desire that lights the passion your employees want to feel. It emanates from you and has a significant and powerful impact on all those around you.

To successfully lead from the heart, you have to care about what you do. That means being concerned not just about money, power, and perks, but about doing something meaningful, making a difference, and changing things for the better.

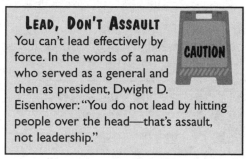

LEAD, DON'T ASSAULT
You can't lead effectively by force. In the words of a man who served as a general and then as a president, Dwight D. Eisenhower: "You do not lead by hitting people over the head—that's assault, not leadership."

If you care about what you're doing, the hard work and stress are less likely to wear you down. The same holds true for your employees.

Use your caring to motivate your employees to care—about their work, about each other, about the organization. Lead from the heart to build a team of employees focused on working together to achieve their goals.

Teambuilding: What's Love Got to Do with It?

A primary human need is to be loved. Translate this into teambuilding and you have a management requirement to care for your people. This is the kind of love that comes from working together to achieve goals.

When you think of leaders who love their people, it's hard not to think of Southwest Airlines' former CEO and president Herb Kelleher. There are plenty of "tough-as-leather" managers out there who would hate to be associated with the word "love" in the workplace. But not Herb. In fact, if you look up Southwest Airlines on the New York Stock Exchange, you'll see that the ticker symbol is LUV.

Successfully building a *loving* team results largely from the *loving* leadership a team has received. But the people on the team are important too. According to Kelleher, "We are always interested in people who externalize, who focus on other people, who are really motivated to help other people."

Having worked with Kelleher firsthand, I can tell you that he is an amazing leader who loves his people. And Herb isn't a guy who just talks the talk about *luv*. I've seen him run across airport terminals to give a big hug to one of Southwest's pilots or customer service reps. No one at Southwest Airlines ever went feeling un-*luved* or unappreciated by its extraordinary leadership team. Maybe that's why they remain the most profitable and highest-performing airline in the world. Oh and by the way, they've never laid off a single employee in 40 years! This is unheard of in the airline industry! Southwest's president and CEO is now Gary C. Kelly, and now having worked with Gary for several years, I can attest that he is spreading the *luv* and taking Herb's legacy to a whole new level of employee motivation and inspiration! It seems, "Just plane smart," as some employees would say!

ON NOT WASTING OUR LIVES

Read this comment by James A. Autry in *Love and Profit: The Art of Caring Leadership*: "Work can provide the opportunity for spiritual and personal, as well as financial, growth. If it doesn't, then we're wasting far too much of our lives."

Now, answer this question: Are you allowing your employees to waste far too much of their lives? Or are you trying hard to help them make the most of the time they spend with you?

How Employees Show They're Committed to Each Other

Just as you must care about your employees, you need to inspire them to care about each other. How do you know if this is happening? How do know when your employees are showing *from the heart* that they're committed to the well-being of others on the team?

Here are a few things to look for:

- Teammates inconvenience themselves to help each other.
- Teammates demonstrate patience and concern for each other.
- Teammates consider love and caring an act of will; they choose to do it.
- Teammates enjoy each other's successes and avoid envy and jealousy.
- Teammates show compassion for each other. They can identify with the pain of others, and they're compelled to help relieve it.
- Teammates forgive each other. They believe others will respond to forgiveness with a deep sense of appreciation and a desire to act responsibly.

How well are you inspiring your employees, by your words and your actions, to care about each other? It may take a while to see results, so don't be discouraged. Sometimes behavior that's most natural is hardest because of the effects of conventional work environments. (Why are so many people surprised and even suspicious when they find out about Southwest Airlines? Because it's definitely an exception to "business as usual.")

Manager's Tips for Encouraging a Loving Team

What can you do as a manager to encourage your teammates to care about each other and what they're doing together? Here are some tips:

- **Tip 1.** Don't hold a grudge against an employee. Forgive and help them learn from mistakes. This sets a good example for others on your team.
- **Tip 2.** Practice the Golden Rule.
- **Tip 3.** Show the members of your team that you care about them, as people and as employees.
- **Tip 4.** Recognize that you need your employees to care about you as well.
- **Tip 5.** Caring requires energy. It's a conscious decision you need to make and carry out each day.

Why can love make such a significant difference in how we lead our teams and motivate our teammates? Simply put, "love" in this context means that you're concerned about your people and their success, you feel glad when they succeed, and you help them when they need help.

> **WORKING TOGETHER**   **SMART**
>
>
>
> "Coming together is a beginning; keeping together is progress; working together is success." —Henry Ford   **MANAGING**
>
> Henry Ford understood the importance of motivation and teamwork. He taught the world about the productivity that is possible when workers join together in a common effort.

Why the Emphasis on Teams?

For some organizations, an emphasis on teamwork has emerged because of a need for cross-functional cooperation. In others, the use of teams has been an attempt to compensate for downsizings and reorganizations.

Teams look quite a bit different today than they did years ago. For one thing, we're now more accustomed to empowering teams to act independently and make their own decisions. Managers are saying to teams, *"You decide what needs to get done and then figure out how to do it."*

Teamwork as a process is generally more complex than individual employees working alone. To begin with, when you're working with others, no member of the team can individually decide what to do and how to do it. Second, teamwork can take longer than expected because coming to consensus can slow down the process.

You may be wondering, "Why in the world would I even consider setting up teams?" Thousands of managers have asked this question—and some probably ask it every time they experience difficulties with their teams. The answer to the question is simple: in general, the positive aspects of working in teams outweigh the negative aspects. Here's a quick list of some of the important advantages:

- Employees working together are generally more successful at solving problems.
- People feel more energized when they are members of a team.
- Teams can make constructive use of differences in expertise, experience, and personalities.
- Team members can better work together to improve processes and reduce waste and costs.
- Teams give employees a sense of belonging and security.
- Teams simply make sense since most work requires the cooperation of employees.

Transforming a group of individuals into a team provides unification and a common sense of interest and direction. But whether your team is permanent or temporary, leading the people on the team to a successful outcome requires skill and finesse on your part.

Let's take a look at how you can go about building a foundation for your team's success. Keep in mind that, as the manager, you set the tone. Your actions and attitudes greatly affect the environment in which your team must perform. From the start, it's important for you to prepare your team for *success*.

10 Ways to Prepare Your Team for Success

1. Give teams a clearly defined goal and purpose.
2. Let the team make its own rules.
3. Encourage fun and a sense of humor on the job.
4. Give employees the authority to make decisions and act on them.
5. Be supportive. Do what you say you'll do.
6. Let the team find solutions to its problems without intervening.
7. Allow team members to make financial decisions and create their own budgets.
8. Expect ups and downs. Some phases of a project will run more smoothly than others.
9. Let the team set up a reward system.
10. Create and nourish team spirit and pride.

Team Spirit Unifies

The last of the 10 suggestions for preparing your team for success is "create and nourish team spirit and pride." Successful teams have spirit. Team spirit is cohesive, energizing, and compelling. It brings everyone together to work toward a common goal.

You can be a more motivating manager by not only instilling spirit in your team, but also by showing it yourself. You can positively influence your employees' motivation and morale by showing that you believe in your team and by supporting it.

We're all familiar with team spirit in sports. But how does it work in business? Let's take an example.

USAA is the pride of San Antonio, Texas. And it's no wonder. The provider of financial services to members of the U.S. military knows how to keep employee spirit and morale alive. USAA has gained a reputation for employee dedication in an environment that's somewhat unconventional in the insurance and banking industries. In fact, this military-focused financial services company is growing so fast that banks like Chase and Wells Fargo are sitting up and taking notice.

USAA supports its employees' team spirit in very real ways. The Fortune 500 company extended employee benefits to domestic partners this year and boasts several on-site child care centers, and some 80 percent of the

> **FOR EXAMPLE**
>
> ### ENCOURAGING TEAM SPIRIT
>
> When we talk about team spirit, we usually connect the idea with sports. It's usually just an analogy.
>
> But it's more than that at SAS, a leader in the business analytics software and services industry and listed No. 1 by *Fortune* magazine as one of America's Best Companies to Work For (January 2011). SAS motivates workers and shows its winning team spirit in the software industry by providing employees with a 66,000-square-foot gym, car cleaning, high-quality childcare, a beauty salon, and summer camp for kids. Maybe you can't provide such facilities and opportunities. But you can develop other ways for teams to play as well as work.

company's employees work only four-day weeks. USAA is also noted for offering its employees the best in-house training programs in the industry. In addition, USAA's 31-acre employee campus has walking trails, jogging trails, and three state-of-the-art fitness centers. Spirit at this company is alive and well—and so are the company's profits!

Maybe you can't provide your employees with child care centers, four-day weeks, and in-house training. But you can learn a lesson from this forward-thinking enterprise—in particular, from its commitment to a motivating and spirited list of "PRIDE Principles," which include the following:

- Exceed customer expectations.
- Be a leader.
- Participate and contribute.
- Pursue excellence.
- Work as a team.
- Share knowledge.
- Keep it simple.
- Listen and communicate.
- Have fun.

Google It

In a day where Google has swept our lives by integrating our calendars, e-mail, and even infiltrated many of our cell phones, we might wonder how they did it. Besides some great technology, Google, ranked in *Fortune's*

2011 Best Places to Work, is committed to fostering a fun and healthy teamwork setting. According to their website, "Though Google has grown a lot since it opened in 1998, we still maintain a small company feel. At lunchtime, almost everyone eats in the office café, sitting at whatever table has an opening and enjoying conversations with Googlers from different teams. Our commitment to innovation depends on everyone being comfortable sharing ideas and opinions. Every employee is a hands-on contributor, and everyone wears several hats." In fact, Google has weekly TGIF meetings in which they allow anyone to pose questions to their senior leadership.

Google's main office is actually physically set up for optimal teamwork. They have very few solo offices, instead offering shared cubes, yurts, and huddle rooms. They offer scooters and bicycles to use for travel from meeting to meeting, and permit dogs and eclectic décor like large inflatable balls and lava lamps. Large murals display local scenes. Their café stocks healthy foods. They show they care about keeping individuals and teams happy!

From HR Thought Leader to Cheerleader

Stephanie Montanez has been dubbed one of California's HR thought leaders, as well as a subject-matter expert, when it comes to improving employee performance through a variety of tried-and-true methods. Her philosophy is to improve performance, and avoid employee performance hurdles, by using a "Praise in Progress Methodology" along with effective formal "Employee Coaching and Development Plans." Montanez is director of human resources at America's leader in the healthcare medical billing industry, MedAmerica Billing Services, Inc. (MBSI), located in Modesto, California.

In her leadership position, Montanez also created a highly successful Employee Development and Coaching division for more than 600 employees, with locations throughout California and Arizona.

According to Montanez, managers must become cheerleaders for their employees. She states that she's mentored some supervisors and managers who operate on a "glass half empty" approach, and they can suck the life out of an organization. She gives leaders tools to combat that way of thinking and enable them to operate on a "glass half full" approach. Her philosophy on operating on a "glass half full" approach will bring life to a stagnant business that needs an uplift of cheer.

Everyone Needs Someone in Their Cheering Gallery

According to Montanez, "Everyone needs a cheerleader, and your employees need cheering from you most of all. This helps to keep them motivated to work to their potential and take ownership in the work when completed. Cheerleading has always been a part of positive motivation that can move a team or individual to the next level.

"As leaders of an organization, it is your responsibility to lead the employees to success and to help them become the best that they can be. Employees at times need to be pushed up to the next level."

Montanez explains the C-H-E-E-R acronym that she uses to help leaders keep their employees motivated and working as a high performing work team:

C – Capture them doing something right.

H – Help them succeed by developing their talent.

E – Envision their future success and help them to buy into it.

E – Encourage success even when they are discouraged.

R – Recognize individual positive actions and performance.

Capture Them Doing Something Right

Capturing an employee doing something right is a key concept to remember when trying to motivate your employees. If the only feedback you give your employees is negative, then you will have a difficult time motivating them and keeping them motivated to sustain excellent performance.

> **KEY TERM**
> **Praise** To commend; to applaud; to express approval of—applied to a person or his or her acts or actions. This approval increases the employee's self-worth and helps motivate the employee to do more!

"Capture the little things as well as the big things and make a big deal about it. Even if you feel that it is 'just their job,' *praise* them anyway. A little praise goes a long way. Praise is a positive reinforcement that all employees crave," says Montanez.

Constant praise increases self-worth and employees who feel worthy and appreciated are more productive and motivated to do a great job. As all great leaders know, "people" are the organization's greatest assets and can either uphold a business or help it fail. The toughest part of a leader's job is to sustain excellence even in a down economy. Becoming your employees' cheerleader can keep your business successful!

Help Them Succeed by Developing Their Talent

"Employees do not care about what you know until they know that you care about them," says Montanez. "Part of caring about them is training and developing their talents, skills, and abilities."

Montanez goes on to say, "When you help to develop their talent, the employees feel you care about their success and have a vested interest in them as a people. When employees meet small goals, assign them additional projects that emphasize their strengths in accomplishing a goal.

"Keep training alive and vivid, not dull and boring. Think of motivating games that help employees learn new concepts. The MedAmerica Billing Services, Inc. (MBSI) training department developed a Jeopardy game to infuse fun and teach key terms and concepts at the same time. Individuals can compete against their fellow trainees for prizes for winning the game. A little healthy competition helps employees reach higher goals to 'beat' their coworkers and win big! When your employees win, so do you. When you win so does the organization," adds Montanez.

Envision Their Future Success and Help Them Buy into It

Creating *vision* for your employees is a key to success. Employees need to be able to visualize themselves being successful in order to succeed. When you discuss vision with your employees, always talk as if it's already a success. "Show your employees where they can be in 1 year, 5 years, and in 20 years, if they work hard and shoot for the moon—even if they miss—they'll land among the stars," says Montanez. She adds that people in general cannot do anything that they feel that they cannot do. If you encourage them, train them in the skills that they need to be suc-

Vision The act or power of anticipating that which will or may come to be.

KEY TERM

cessful and help them to reach their goals, they will be committed to you and help you succeed.

Encourage Success Even When They Are Discouraged

All people need encouragement to be successful. Think back to your younger years and imagine one defining moment of your life. Most likely this defining moment was when someone encouraged you when you felt you could go no further. Being the ultimate cheerleader for your employees and giving them the encouragement that they need, especially in times of crises, will go a long way.

Many managers make the mistake of only recognizing and encouraging the team and not the individual. They may say that they want to be consistent and not appear to show favoritism. While these perceptions can exist, you should be challenged to encourage the *individual* instead of the entire team. When you do this, the real magic begins, and you create a bond with the employee. Employees feel that you notice them for their individual efforts and didn't just lump them in with the team.

Recognize Individual Positive Actions and Performance

"When leaders recognize positive actions and performance, it drives home positive morale, self-worth, and increases productivity," says Montanez. "This is a jump-start on the road of success for the individual, team, and organization. There is a common misconception that there is no 'I' in team. This is not true; without each person's individual talents, skills, abilities, and efforts no 'team' would exist. As leaders, you need to cherish the fact that 'not everyone is just like me.' If everyone was just like us, the world would just sit still. By tapping into individual talents, providing positive individual recognition, and understanding the way to communicate with your employees, you are leading everyone to the road of success. Think of it as a pathway following a rainbow and reaching the pot of gold at the end. Your employees are that pot of gold and you have the golden opportunity to lead them to success."

Montanez's tried-and-true concepts on motivating employees that take the individual, team, and organization to the next level can be found at HumanResourcesSources.org.

> ### Free Monthly HR Ideas and Motivation Tips
> HumanResourcesSources.org is a highly regarded and popular human resources website where HR professionals can go to get free, downloadable worksheets and forms for solving HR employee problems, just-in-time, cutting-edge techniques and tools from interviews, teleseminars, webinars, MP3 downloads, Podcasts, articles, white papers, one-sheets, and more—plus listen in on motivational broadcasts worldwide.
>
> **TOOLS**
>
> HumanResourcesSources.org showcases dozens of effective training programs on the art of leadership, motivating and developing superstar talent, coaching for success, communications excellence, employee development planning, harnessing the power of emotional and social intelligence, and also features details on one of their most popular seminars for HR professionals—*HR from the Head and Heart.*

Next Man Up Management

Coach Tony Dungy, who is a Super Bowl champion both as a player and a coach, is known for his "next man up" method of coaching. What this means is he treats each player on the team as if he has equal importance. He stated, "My attitude was to try to show everyone on the team that their role was critical to us winning, to treat everyone with respect. I think if the leader does that, that transmits to other players, as opposed to saying, 'Well, these people are important, these are less important, these people are not at all.'" Similarly, if applied to management, the next man up philosophy empowers every team member to give his or her best, and to feel part of achieving the goals and contributing to the success of the organization.

Affinity Groups, Employee Resource Groups, and Inclusion Meetings Create a Twenty-First Century Workplace

In today's world, we have more diversity than ever. There are no communities or groups of people that are not diverse—no matter how small or large; even if by their appearance it may not be apparent, everyone is unique. When we deal with difficult people, encounter accidental collisions, argue, whisper, and giggle about others who operate outside our map of the world, it's often because we're making assumptions about people and not respecting someone else's one-of-a-kind contributions.

Perhaps we only see the exterior—subconsciously profiling people who look and act like they are from another place and then using insensitive and inappropriate labels to describe them. Social science often shows us that our individual beliefs about equality may indeed cause major problems in the workplace, including lost revenues and decreased productivity.

"You're awesome girl ... you're awesome!"—Oprah Winfrey on Vernice Amour. Managers who are serious about diversity may wish to bring in an expert to speak on the subject and motivate their teams with something, or someone, fresh and new. Vernice Armour is one such speaker (and the author of *Zero to Breakthrough)* who shares her strategies on breaking through fear, valuing our differences, and moving forward. She's the first female African-American who went from beat cop to combat pilot for the Marines in just three years. Now there's a woman who's broken the mold! Additionally, as she speaks and teaches, organizations are creating excitement, retention, and engagement among their employees by developing employee resource groups (ERGs) and affinity groups for special interests, such as African-American groups, Asian-American groups, women in leadership, valor (men and women returning to the workforce from the military), physically challenged individuals, or gay and lesbian groups.

These important "inclusion groups," as they are sometimes referred to, allow individuals to value their differences while assisting their companies in strategic marketing, product development, and helping with the retention of talented workers—who come from every walk of life—all contributors, all potential leaders, motivated to share their special talents, stories, and competencies from their maps of the world. Companies are quickly seeing the value of these special-interest groups and are hosting meetings for everyone to come together so all can be on the same page with the same mission, building tolerance, sharing ideas, and growing acceptance of others. It's the new, twenty-first century diversity, and it's a new way to view and take advantage of the diversity of today's workforce.

Mosaic Mentors Motivates Managers to Take Action On Diversity

Diversity training is making its way into industries across the gamut of industries. One such company that addresses this need, Mosaic Mentors, is the only speakers bureau specializing in this niche of diversity and inclusion meetings. Betty Garrett and Michele Lucia are collaborating on this venture because as businesspeople of women-owned businesses, they've experienced many challenges climbing the corporate ladder, owning their own businesses, and balancing their personal lives.

They understand the hurdles, frustrations, and obstacles many of the ERG members experience. Because of their backgrounds, they're better able to understand the needs, as well as save time, energy, and stress when an organization needs a speaker, trainer, consultant, or coach for each ERG. They've been matching the perfect speaker to the right audiences for more than a combined 60 years and are considered experts in their fields. Check out their website at www.MosaicMentors.com for additional information on how you can motivate your unique, one-of-a-kind teams and special groups with a speaker or trainer who is sensitive to your organization's culture, people, and their special interests.

Tips for Starting Up Affinity Groups, ERGs, and Inclusion Councils

- **Engage management.** Affinity networks need the support of senior management to be effective.
- **Cast a wide net.** Don't focus on headquarters; create regional networks and affinity groups in your field offices. Isolated or home-based employees can be conferenced in.
- **Recruit passionate people.** Affinity networks should be composed of volunteers—enthusiastic ones.
- **Be targeted.** Identify your network's purpose and goals and set strategies to accomplish them.
- **Get a sponsor.** Enlist an understanding advisor or sponsor from senior management who can represent your group to management and carry messages the other way.
- **Start small.** It's better to focus on tasks that the group can accom-

plish. Once it has a few successes, the team can work its way up to more ambitious goals.

- **Connect with other networks.** The purpose of affinity networks is to eliminate barriers and isolation. Create alliances with other affinity networks to increase their knowledge and influence.
- **Be open.** To open doors, the group needs to extend favors to others.
- **Measure progress.** Benchmark the network's accomplishments against stated goals. If it is falling short, redouble efforts or recalibrate priorities.
- **Communicate.** Announce meetings throughout the company and welcome new members. Share accomplishments and insights.
- **Collaborate effectively.** Create a positive approach with management to ensure that plans are win-win.

The Motivational Benefits of Affinity Groups

Affinity groups have many benefits that motivate teams. Here are a few:

- Infuse recruitment and retention efforts.
- Broaden employee awareness.
- Create ways to be comfortable with people different than ourselves.
- Embrace differences and agree to disagree agreeably when called for.
- Reduce costs of replacing key executives.
- Aid training and development on many levels.
- Improve morale and boost motivation.
- Build links to special-interest markets.
- Provide fresh ideas.
- Improve internal communications.
- Provide a feedback mechanism to corporations on key opportunities.
- Help discover hidden talent.
- Promote advancement of women and minorities.
- Provide a mechanism for community involvement.
- Promote understanding and bring company employees closer together.

Managing Self-Directed Teams

In general, the longer team members work together, the more effective the team becomes. As relationships develop, they contribute to a unified effort

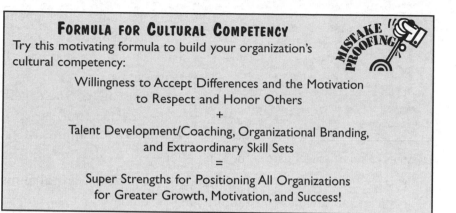

FORMULA FOR CULTURAL COMPETENCY

Try this motivating formula to build your organization's cultural competency:

Willingness to Accept Differences and the Motivation
to Respect and Honor Others

+

Talent Development/Coaching, Organizational Branding,
and Extraordinary Skill Sets

=

Super Strengths for Positioning All Organizations
for Greater Growth, Motivation, and Success!

that pulls everyone together in getting the job done. When this happens, it almost becomes second nature for the team to perform at higher and higher levels. Through working together, employees learn how to become a more productive unit. They also learn to do more for themselves.

YOU CAN'T IMPOSE SPIRIT

Resist the temptation to do too much for your teams and for team spirit.

CAUTION

Team spirit cannot be top-down, imposed on people. If it smells of a management technique, it's likely to fail. So let your teams decide what they need and ask you to provide it. Don't smother them with support—or you risk giving the impression that you're trying to control.

Team spirit comes from working well together and identifying with other team members, the team as a whole, and its purpose. You can't impose any of that; you can only help create the environment where it emerges.

They learn how to take initiative, not only to solve problems and take advantage of opportunities to improve, but even to anticipate problems and seek out opportunities. As time passes, the employees require less managing from you, until they become essentially a self-directed team.

But what do you do as a manager when your employees are managing themselves as teams? Basically, you support those teams.

Supporting Self-Directed Work Teams

If you decide to allow your teams to do their thing, congratulations—and condolences. It's like letting your kid go off to school for the first time.

KEY TERM

Self-directed work team A team that manages its own affairs without any direct supervision. It's completely in charge of all activities involved in the processes for which it is responsible.

You want to be there, to help, but you realize it's best just to back off and hope it will all work out OK.

Fortunately, there are some specific strategies you can use to improve the chances of success. Here are some suggestions:

- Discuss the concept of the self-managed team, particularly in terms of the responsibilities and authority of its members.
- Explain the rationale behind working as *self-directed teams*.
- Agree mutually on criteria for success.
- Support team leaders with ongoing encouragement.
- Keep providing positive feedback. Focus on the successes, which can further motivate team members.
- Emphasize what your employees can gain from working together as a self-directed team.

Inspiring Creativity in Teams

Contrary to popular belief, creativity isn't necessarily spontaneous, nor does it come from a gene we inherit. In actuality, we sometimes have to *plan* to be spontaneous.

Give employees a time and a place to practice their creative thinking. Soon, everyone will become more creative and help in the brainstorming process.

When you get employees to think "outside the box" and use their imaginations, they find solutions to problems they (or you) never knew they

TRICKS OF THE TRADE

TEAMWORK

Here's a creative idea: develop your own team acronym.

Here's an example, using the word "teamwork":

Together
Everyone
Accomplishes
More
With
Organization,
Responsibility, and
Knowledge

We don't recommend an acronym for every team. But it can often help unite, focus, and motivate team members.

had. Employees create amazingly helpful, efficient, and even profitable ideas we never dreamed possible. Teamwork and creativity go hand in hand.

Teams, Teams, Teams

As we noted at the start of this chapter, business depends on people and on their relationships. They are the heart and the soul, the brains and the muscle in our systems, as we stressed in Chapter 9. Smart managers know how to take advantage of the many benefits of cultivating those relationships and of using them to motivate their employees.

Maybe you can help your employees develop self-directed teams. If so, that's great. But you may not be able to do that in your environment. You can, however, try to build the sense of community among your employees. That can be a powerful force that motivates each of them to try a little harder, to be a little smarter, to do more and to do it better. That feeling of community is the essence of inspiring motivated teamwork.

Manager's Checklist for Chapter 10

☑ Business is about people and the relationships they develop. Smart managers foster the teamwork that makes individuals into a community and motivates them to do more.

☑ Teamwork helps people perform better. There are two keys to teamwork as it relates to motivation: making a difference and caring about people. The desire to make a difference encourages us to focus on the big picture and endure the challenges of working with people. Caring motivates us to find value in working with others and in relationships.

☑ Motivating managers care about leading, about people, and about what their organizations do. That caring comes through in their relationships with their employees.

☑ Psychologists claim that our strongest need is to be loved. If you want to create effective teamwork, you must care for your people, encouraging them and inspiring them by your caring words and actions.

☑ To instill teamwork, you've got to have team spirit, the cohesive, energizing, and compelling force that brings individuals together to work toward a common goal. You can further motivate your team and build teamwork by allowing your employees the initiative to handle new jobs or solve critical problems. Encourage and inspire creative thinking: teamwork and creativity go hand in hand.

☑ Practice the C-H-E-E-R Acronym:

  C – Capture them doing something right.

  H – Help them succeed by developing their talent.

  E – Envision their future success and help them to buy into it.

  E – Encourage success even when they are discouraged.

  R – Recognize individual positive actions and performance.

☑ Tap into free downloadable HR worksheets and real-world conversations and forms for helping solve employee performance problems at HumanResourcesSources.org. Get free, just-in-time, monthly training tools for motivating and developing top talent in your organization and view highlights of showcased training programs and seminars, including one for HR pros called *HR from the Head and Heart.*

Unleash the Potential of Synergy

It All Comes Down to Movement and Momentum

Your brain's capacity is practically unfathomable. In terms of its intricacies and power, the brain surpasses even the latest technology: it can process up to 30 billion bits of information per second through the equivalent of more than 6,000 miles of computer wiring. The fuel that fires up your brain is pretty simple: oxygen in your blood and a little glucose.

Synergism occurs when your nervous system works together with your brain through an amazing network of 100,000 miles of nerve fibers. Through this network, composed of billions upon billions of neurons, your nervous system interprets the information received by your organs and conveys it to your brain, which then sends instructions to your muscles.

It's a synergistic miracle. All the parts of the system work together to accomplish amazing feats every moment.

Now, think about your employees. As a manager and leader, you have the opportunity to unleash their synergistic potential. Your employees are equipped with all the right wiring in their brains. You simply have to tap into that synergistic energy to produce the results you seek.

This chapter looks at some of the ways you can encourage and develop the motivating power of *synergy* in your organization.

KEY TERM

Synergy This is the result of interactions that make the whole greater than the sum of its parts. In other words, the members of a team accomplish more together than they would separately.

You can promote synergy by bringing together individuals who are diverse in their abilities and experiences, and by helping them develop a healthy environment where they feel comfortable in both conflict and cooperation.

Team Members Develop the Potential in Others

Working side by side with one another: it's a great way for your employees to learn, to coach and be coached, and to get inspired to do their best. Unfortunately, with reengineering and downsizing, we sacrifice a sense of community among employees—even if we work at developing teams, as recommended in Chapter 10. A smart manager, though, still finds ways to build community and to inspire synergy.

When people work in teams or one-on-one, you have an opportunity to help them bring out their best. In fact, synergism can occur even when workers simply observe other workers, watching them do things right over and over. It's motivating to watch success in action, and it instills a sense of confidence—"Hey, if she can do it, so can I." The next thing you know, the effects are cumulative and momentum has developed.

Isn't that what you really want? You want to foster that sense of community. You want to inspire and breed that synergy, You want to encourage that feeling that builds an environment where people can feel good things happening, where they feel compelled to jump in and get involved in their work community.

Success Breeds Success

Success breeds success. We all accept that truism, but we don't generally think about why it's true. So, let's look at the story of 10-year-old Sam and his experience in Little League baseball.

The season was nearly over. Sam was devastated. Once again he'd struck out. He was upset, although not really surprised. After all, he'd gone the whole season without a hit. He left the plate sobbing, not only embarrassed but completely frustrated. He'd had it with Little League.

Next up at bat was Sam's best friend, Marty, who also had yet to get a hit. A few moments later, Marty had struck out as well and was slowly walking back to the bench. He plopped down in utter disappointment next to Sam.

On the drive home, Sam's mom tried to console Sam and Marty. "Boys, it's only a game. You did the best you could." Sam's dad concurred.

Then Sam burst out, "No, it's not! I can't hit the ball! Don't you know that Marty and me are the only guys on the team who haven't had a hit all year? At school they tease us and call us names. We feel like a couple of losers." Marty sat there silently.

That's when Sam's dad made a suggestion. "OK, boys. There are three more games left in the season. So this is what we're gonna do. Starting tomorrow after school, we're going to do one thing and one thing only all afternoon. We're gonna practice hitting that ball. That's all, just hitting the ball. What do you say?"

Both boys thought this sounded like a plan that might help, and so they agreed.

The next afternoon, right after school, Sam and Marty met Sam's dad at the park. He then started teaching the boys everything he knew about hitting a baseball.

> **START COACHING EARLY**
>
> Don't wait for your employees to fail. Start coaching them from the beginning. It's always easier to prepare for success when you haven't been hurt by failures. Don't assume that your employees need your help, but don't wait until they prove it either. Being a good coach requires sensitivity and tact.

"OK, Marty, give me a nice level swing. Thatta boy. Do it again. Watch the ball, Sam. Don't try to clobber it. Keep it steady. Watch the ball meet the bat."

This went on for hours every day after school. Finally the weekend came, with another Little League game.

Marty surprised everyone by hitting a double. As he stood at second base, he was grinning from ear to ear, obviously loving it.

Sam's dad felt pretty good, too. Then he suddenly realized how awful it would be if his own son didn't get a hit as well. He prayed Sam would remember the coaching he'd provided.

It was now Sam's turn at bat. The first pitch came and he barely missed it. The second pitch was a strike. Sam stood there, just one pitch away from another failure.

"Please," thought his dad, "remember what I taught you."

On the next pitch, Sam hit a home run! As both boys rounded third base and headed for home plate, their teammates came off the bench, cheering uncontrollably. And the team went on to win the game.

The Moral of the Story: Why Not Me?

On the way home, Sam's dad stopped for an ice cream celebration. He felt pretty pleased with himself. "I'm sure proud of you boys. Wow, a double and a home run! That goes to show you what great coaching can do, huh?"

Sam looked at his dad as if to say, "You don't get it, do you, dad?"

Sam's dad was puzzled. He asked again what the boys thought about his coaching.

"Well, dad," Sam blurted out, "we really appreciated your help. But your coaching had nothing to do with why I hit that home run. It's just that when I saw Marty hit the double I said to myself, 'If Marty can hit the ball, then so can I.'"

The moral of this story is that no matter how much you may coach or mentor your employees, they've got to want to succeed and they've got to believe in themselves. When Sam saw Marty get a hit, he suddenly believed. He thought, "Why not me?" That confidence turned his desire into the motivation he needed.

SMART MANAGING

THE DESIRE TO EXCEL

Remember that all motivation is intrinsic. The desire to excel on the job (or not) comes from within. Focus your energies on encouraging that desire in your employees by providing opportunities to learn and perform—and excel!

What was the effect of the coaching? We'll never know. But a good coach doesn't care about taking credit. What matters is how the players perform and how they feel motivated to succeed.

If you give employees abundant encouragement and support, they will believe they can succeed. Then each success will breed more success, as they synergistically build a momentum of realizing their potential.

Benchmark to Inspire Synergy

It's easy to understand how Sam might think, watching Marty get a hit, "I can do that, too." That reaction is natural in all of us, at any age, in any circumstance. As a manager, you can apply this understanding with great results, by observing other departments or other organizations that are doing something exceptionally well and *benchmarking* against them.

In one company, two managers of a call center spent an entire afternoon listening in on telephone interviews being conducted by one of the supervisors in the organization. At the end of the day, both managers were motivated and eager to try the same technique as soon as possible. They couldn't get over how their observation of this process actually inspired them to do some very creative brainstorming and out-of-the-box thinking. Both managers came away with the conclusion, "If that supervisor can do this, so can we!"

When you benchmark best practices by obtaining information—researching and analyzing various sources—there are two major benefits. The first benefit is the one that generally comes to mind: you can find ways to improve the quality in your own organization. The second benefit is a bonus: benchmarking can fire up the motivation of your employees.

Here are some steps you can take to help your employees establish a benchmarking program:

> **Benchmarking** This is a method for learning from the example of others. You first identify work units or **KEY TERM** entire organizations that excel. Then you collect and analyze information on the processes of those units or organizations from various sources, either internal or external. Based on your comparisons, you draw conclusions about ways to improve your own processes.

Step 1. Create a benchmarking team. Select employees to act as a team. You'll want to bring together people who have organizational abilities and analytical skills and who can think flexibly and creatively. To lead the team, choose someone who has credibility in the organization and the ability to work well with people from outside organizations.

Step 2. Explain the purpose of benchmarking. As with any activities, your employees should know why they're doing the work. Make sure they understand the purpose of benchmarking. It's not to simply imitate another organization, but rather to adapt what you learn about that organization to fit your own situation.

Step 3. Plan a strategy. Make a list. Get organized. Focusing on your purpose for benchmarking, decide on what, who, where, when, and how. What information will the team be requesting? From whom, either internally or externally? Who will do what? Where? When? How will this information be gathered—by telephone, fax, e-mail, personal appointment, or surveys? How will it be shared with the other members of the team?

KNOW YOUR OWN PROCESSES FIRST

CAUTION Beware of the temptation to go shopping when you don't know what's in your own cupboards. In other words, know what you're doing and how you're doing it before you go off in search of ways to improve.

The time you invest in studying your current processes will be well worth it. You'll have a better idea of what you need, where you might find it, and how to make the most of it once you have it.

Step 4. Take inventory of your present situation. Ask the team to perform an assessment of your department or your organization, to uncover all the information on all the subjects that will be necessary for the benchmarking effort. Before they start benchmarking, team members must understand the importance of the information to be collected.

Step 5. Think broadly. Don't limit yourself to industry leaders. Get information from direct competitors and aspiring, growth-oriented organizations. (You can find this information by reading their ads and other sales information, by purchasing their products, by talking with people from other companies, through skyping, social media, like Facebook and LinkedIn, and by searching the Web.) Do your competitors perform critical functions consistent with the best practices in your industry? Try to uncover the reasons behind any competitive advantages or disadvantages.

Step 6. Benchmark best practices of industries outside your own. Some of the best benchmarking will come from outside your industry. If you're in banking, encourage the team to benchmark an airline. If you're in manufacturing, try benchmarking a food distributor. Contrary to popular belief, best practices are often transferred between diverse industries, and with measurable success. If you think only about *what* you do, you're likely to see *obstacles*.

> **"THANKS FOR THE HELP"** **SMART**
>
> Always thank any organizations that provide information for your benchmarking effort by giving them an overall sum- **MANAGING** mary of your findings. Of course, you should always maintain the confidentiality of each organization.

But if you think about *how* you do what you do and how you can learn from others to improve, you'll find *opportunities*.

Step 7. Share what you've discovered with those who gave you the information. Thank those who are kind enough to share with you the best practices of their organizations. Give them a summary of your benchmarking results. Be sure to maintain the confidentiality of each organization benchmarked.

Step 8. Make benchmarking a habit. Benchmarking should not be just a one-shot effort. It's a great way to keep up with the best in the business, as well as the best practices. Try new organizations. Don't wear out your welcome at one particular organization. And, of course, if an organization wants to contact you for benchmarking, take it as a compliment—then extend the same courtesy as you expected from others.

> **SKYPE OR USE SOCIAL MEDIA FIRST**
>
> Benchmark by skyping, using social media, e-mailing, or telephoning to save time. You **TOOLS** can get results immediately when you interview by phone, Skype, or e-mail. This technique also offers the opportunity to build relationships. Making a new business contact is an extra bonus of telephone or Skype interviewing.

Once your benchmarking team has accumulated and analyzed the data it has gathered, it should publicize the results throughout your organization. Encourage the team to get ideas from other employees and managers. This is the essence of knowledge management. It's also a good way to encourage organizational learning, which has a positive overall impact on employee motivation.

Use All Those Brains Around You

When employees gather and share information, and when they exchange ideas and suggestions, the synergistic momentum builds. Smart managers find ways to encourage this natural development.

> **SMART MANAGING**
>
> ### START WITH YOUR EMPLOYEES
>
> Walmart founder Sam Walton once noted: "The key to success is to get out into the store and listen to what the associates have to say. It's terribly important for everyone to get involved. Our best ideas come from clerks and stockers."

Have you ever wondered why employees in some organizations send a flood of ideas to upper management, while in other companies the suggestion box is covered with dust? What's the difference? It's not necessarily the employees, but the organizational culture—whether or not the employees feel encouraged to open up and share new ideas, safely and without ridicule, confident that their suggestions will be respected and welcomed.

Here are some ways you can continue to encourage great ideas from employees:

- **Ask . . . and keep asking.** Don't give up. Tell employees you really do want to hear their suggestions. After a while, they'll believe you, especially when they see you use their ideas.
- **Don't offer your opinions right away.** Even if you mean well, that reaction may intimidate some employees. Give them a chance to offer their suggestions first. Ask them questions that invite them to express their ideas more fully.
- **Focus on a specific area.** Sometimes the freedom of being encouraged to think can overwhelm employees, especially if they're not used to managers who encourage thinking. To start them off, you may want to choose a certain process or problem for them to think about.
- **Have a better-faster-more-affordable contest.** Ask for ideas on how to improve things in the organization. Request suggestions on how to speed up processes and save money, for example. Offer first, second, and third prizes for those with the best solutions.
- **Be timely in reacting to employees' suggestions.** We all want feed-

back—and the sooner we get it, the more we feel reassured about offering our ideas. Don't get in a position where employees are saying, "Gee, I wonder what ever happened to that idea I suggested two months ago?" Respond quickly, even if only to let that person know you're considering the idea.

■ **Assure employees that you're all thinking together.** Employees feel their suggestions have greater value when they're on the same wavelength as you. Share your goals. Explain your vision.

You can use these ideas and others to create your own system for employee suggestions. This can take any form you desire. You can set out the traditional box or create an e-mail address. Get creative, publicize your input system, and make it easy for people to participate. Be sure you have your boss's support, and assure your employees that there's no danger of retribution if they're critical of a current process and have suggestions for improving it. After all, that's the whole point of seeking suggestions in the first place.

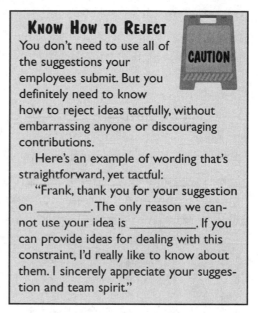

KNOW HOW TO REJECT

You don't need to use all of the suggestions your employees submit. But you definitely need to know how to reject ideas tactfully, without embarrassing anyone or discouraging contributions.

Here's an example of wording that's straightforward, yet tactful:

"Frank, thank you for your suggestion on _____. The only reason we cannot use your idea is _____. If you can provide ideas for dealing with this constraint, I'd really like to know about them. I sincerely appreciate your suggestion and team spirit."

Unfortunately, your good intentions and reassurances may not convince some employees. You can't overcome immediately the effects of bad experiences elsewhere. If that's the case, you could offer to take their suggestions and transmit them to the appropriate personnel anonymously. That way, they risk nothing. Then, as they realize their fears are ungrounded, they'll be convinced. Every employee has a brain. How many are you now using—and to what extent?

You can unleash the potential in employees if you create an environment where they can flourish, get swift feedback and recognition, and earn rewards for their good ideas.

THE BEST REWARDS

How should you reward employees whose suggestions you use? It may mean the most to employees to see their suggestions put to use and to receive public recognition for their contributions. Then, it's nice to receive symbolic awards, such as T-shirts, certificates, plaques, and special pins. Other possibilities are a lunch for the team or dinner for two on the company, or fancy gift cards that you can easily pick up almost anywhere for any value good for iTunes, shopping, and even travel! Finally, cash awards are a possibility, with the amount depending on the financial benefit to the organization.

Here's something to try: Ask your employees. Do you guess that they'll all want cash? Don't be too sure about that. Just ask them.

Possess the "Eyes to See" Your Employees

Each year, many leaders set goals and intentions. Marlene Chism, speaker and author of *Stop Workplace Drama*, says that an important goal of any leader is to request, "Give me the eyes to see." What the physical eyes see is only part of the story. As a leader, you can influence others and foster synergy if you're willing to see or envision your employees beyond their immediate roles.

Here are three examples from Chism of how you can look for and encourage the best in others by having the *eyes to see*:

1. See Your Employees' Brilliance. "Isn't it a relief that as a leader, you do not have to rely on doing it all yourself? You can rely on the brilliance of others. I realized this recently when I recognized how grateful I was for the brilliance on my team," states Chism. We don't have to be the best at everything. We have brilliant team members who can catch our grammatical errors, connect us with other brilliant partners, or

BRILLIANCE REQUIREMENT

To see the brilliance in others, you have to give up the need to get all the glory, and you have to let others step into the spotlight.

offer ideas to help us improve our processes. If technology is not your thing, what a timesaver it is to no longer have to keep up with the latest technology tips and techniques because your team members have all the brilliance you need! Seeing the brilliance and recognizing it in others will save you time and increase your productivity.

2. See Through Your Employees' Masks. We human beings are odd creatures. When we feel vulnerable, fearful, or threatened in any way, we put on a mask to protect ourselves. When we feel incompetent, we overcompensate, sometimes by lashing out. When an employee irritates us

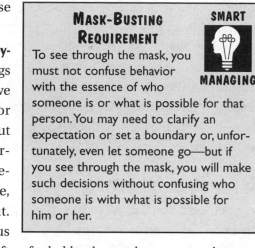

MASK-BUSTING REQUIREMENT

SMART

MANAGING

To see through the mask, you must not confuse behavior with the essence of who someone is or what is possible for that person. You may need to clarify an expectation or set a boundary or, unfortunately, even let someone go—but if you see through the mask, you will make such decisions without confusing who someone is with what is possible for him or her.

or pulls our strings, we are often fooled by the mask we see on that person. If an e-mail is a bit too touchy-feely for our tastes or an employee behaves obnoxiously or uses too much sarcasm, we may be tempted to judge, but we can actually improve synergy. To do that, we need to see beyond those behaviors and into the underlying situation and intentions. This doesn't mean ignore harmful behavior, but instead, step back and see the bigger picture of who and where someone is, and address each person's core needs. When employees feel that you know who they are and what they need, they're more apt to soar with you to the next level.

3. See Your Employees in Relationship to You. The way humans gain confidence is through the mirror of relationship. When you're in a relationship with your employees, you're mutually interested in one another's growth. Your employees hold keys to understanding you from a perspective you can't see, and vice versa. These observations can be the ticket to unleashing entrepreneurial potential. Chism says, "I would still be working in a factory packing cheese, driving a forklift, or doing sanitation on Friday nights if I had not had some loving mirrors reflecting back to me the potential

RELATIONSHIP REQUIREMENT

SMART

MANAGING

To see your employees in relationship to you, you must honor them as people, and discount the story they tell you about why they don't measure up. You must see beyond the current reality and help them hold a vision about what is possible for them.

within." When your employees struggle, empathetically offer perspective on what they cannot see themselves. This motivates employees by helping them to feel supported, capable, and thus empowered to act on goals. If you do not see your employees in relationship to you, but rather as objects to achieve your goals, you contribute to the internal drama that keeps them from being who they came into this world to be. If you do see them this way, and if you foster it, you free them and push them to dream and achieve.

Rejuvenate for Synergy

As a manager, you can get so busy putting out fires that you never invest the necessary time in rejuvenating your organization and your people. Employees burn out. They get tired and things get old.

Creative managers know how to renew the vigor and vitality in employees. Managers who work to renew the energy of their employees are looking to the future and planning for tomorrow.

Here are some suggestions for rejuvenating your employees and creating a rejuvenating work environment in general:

1. Think about the big picture. Help your employees understand their contribution in terms of the entire organization's strategy. Then they'll have a context for thinking more strategically about their individual jobs.

2. Teach innovation. Innovate or abdicate: that's the ultimatum of the business world now. Employees must now do everything better, faster, cheaper, more flexibly, and with more innovation. Get the wheels turning with your own customized innovation program. If there's nobody around your organization to provide that program and you don't want to bring in a trainer, work on coming up with a course on your own. The bookshelves are full of advice on inspiring innovative thinking, such as *A Whack on the Side of the Head* by Roger von Oech and *Manager's Guide to Fostering Innovation and Creativity in Teams* by Charles Prather (another title in the Briefcase Books series). Find out what other organizations are doing to stimulate innovative thinking and try that with your employees.

3. Be compelling. Be upbeat and interesting, speak with personal conviction, have a controversial opinion or two, and speak up so everyone can

> ## DON'T BE COMPLACENT—SUCCESS CAN KILL YOU!
> That may surprise you if you've accepted as truth that line
> about "nothing succeeds like success." Sure, success can breed
> greater success, but not if you become complacent.
>
> CAUTION
>
> Dr. Oliver Wendell Holmes wrote: "The greatest thing in this
> world is not so much where we are, but in what direction we are moving."
> As a leader, you must continue to fight against illusions of security in your
> successes. H. Tom Collard was thinking along those lines when he stated
> that "Success is a journey—not a destination."

hear you. Not everybody can have charisma, but you can certainly open
up your personality.

4. Conquer complacency. Encourage change—and lots of it! Be aggressive
in your battle against complacency. It can kill your organization by drain-
ing the life from your people. When things don't seem broken, there's no
motivation to fix them. So if things seem to be going OK, there's probably
no motivation to improve anything. Don't settle for the status quo, however. If you do, your competitors will likely leave you behind.

5. Praise your employees. Managers are quick to criticize, but not always
so quick to praise. Employees want to know when they're doing things
right and doing the right things. Uplift your employees with genuine and
sincere praise and compliments. Celebrate achievements regularly.

6. Be excited and rejuvenate yourself. Show your feelings in your actions.
Start every day by thinking about several reasons why you enjoy your
work and care about your employees. (If you really can't come up with
any, you definitely need to seek help—or at least take a little vacation!)
Then show how you feel. Get excited. Be the most enthusiastic cheerleader and the greatest fan.

Increase Energy and You Increase Synergy

Without energy, there can be no synergy in your organization. When
people feel tired or listless, they don't accomplish nearly as much as
they're capable of accomplishing. When you work on increasing employees' energy, you help them move toward a better life—not only at work
but in general.

Here are some basic ways you can help employees increase their energy:

- **Encourage your employees to eat properly and take breaks.** When employees skip meals or eat too much, or when they don't take an occasional break, they're missing great opportunities to rejuvenate—and they're bound to wind down. Set a good example. Eat with your employees, and set a good example for them by taking breaks yourself.

- **Encourage your employees to laugh out loud.** When you laugh, you release chemicals in your brain that energize and sustain you. Laughing gives you a physiological boost, not to mention psychological benefits.

- **Encourage your employees to exercise.** This could include in-house aerobics, morning walk teams, or other forms of easy-to-do exercise. It costs very little to exercise people's bodies and minds. Again, serve as a model. Take a quick walk every day and invite your employees to join you. Just 15 or 20 minutes of brisk walking and fresh air can make an incredible difference in how you feel.

- **Encourage your employees to breathe.** That's right, breathe! Sure, it's natural—so natural that we don't take care to do it right. If employees get into the habit of doing deep-breathing exercises during the day, they'll feel a significant difference in their energy levels. Here's an easy exercise: take four or five deep breaths, then hold your breath for a count of five, then release. When you do this, you bring more oxygen into your blood and to your brain, making you feel refreshed and energized almost instantly.

Working Together Is Organic

That's what synergy really means—working together. It's a simple, natural or organic concept—except in business. That's changing, though, as experts stress the importance of "smart work" and "intellectual capital" and as we realize the benefits of teams. It's all about getting people to work together and to use their abilities more fully. The effects on motivation can be amazing!

This chapter has given you some powerful tools for getting the best from your employees. The guidelines and tips offered were meant to get you thinking—thinking about the potential of all your employees, the phenomenal power of all that intelligence, creativity, curiosity, and energy. Make the most of all that potential around you. The results will be well worth your efforts—and the synergy you develop will keep growing, building motivation.

Manager's Checklist for Chapter 11

☑ Find ways to build community among your employees, to inspire synergy (a great way to inspire and motivate).

☑ Encourage and support your employees. When they believe they can succeed, they synergistically begin a momentum of realizing their higher potential.

☑ Help your employees learn from others. Observe other departments or other organizations that are doing something exceptionally well and benchmark against them.

☑ Foster an environment where your employees can open up and share safely and without ridicule, get swift feedback and recognition, and earn rewards for their ideas. Convince employees that their suggestions will be respected and welcomed.

☑ Rejuvenate your employees. Renew their vitality and energy so that they look forward to the future.

☑ Strive to see the brilliance in your employees.

Chapter

12

Conclusion—Driving It All the Way Home

n *The New York Times* bestseller *Drive* (a must-read for all managers)—a book that talks about the surprising things that motivate us—author Daniel Pink draws on four decades of research on the topic of motivation. Pink emphasizes that it's a big mistake for managers to believe that the best way to motivate others is with external rewards, like money. According to Pink, the secret to greater performance and satisfaction—at work, school, or home—is to tap the human need to do better and to direct our own lives. In other words, to be part of something bigger than ourselves, to learn, evolve, and create new and exciting things in our lifetime.

I agree wholeheartedly with Pink and love how he exposes the mismatch between *what science knows and what business often does*. His revelations are transforming and a must-read for managers who want to ignite passion and activate greater potential in their employees and in the workplace.

Be a Success-Oriented Manager

It takes a success-oriented manager to craft solutions and strategies that motivate, inspire, and create environments where people can grow and yield individual and team results. Great managers know and understand the value of celebrating meaningful milestones—work and personal achievements and bigger successes, because they value the contributions of every individual—regardless of their employee's position, tenure, or title.

Create a Sense of Belonging and Greater Purpose

Every day look for ways to honor your employees and kindle their passion for their jobs. Help them to find their greater purpose and potential.

By doing this you'll be further defining and strengthening your organization's culture and designing a feeling of belonging that tells your employees, "You're part of something bigger!"

Dig Deep for Ways to Help Employees Become Self-Motivated

Sometimes a manager has got to dig deep and co-create with his or her employees on ways to tap internal motivation and peak performance. Here are a few suggestions:

- Suggest and inspire ongoing collaboration among workers.
- Suggest real "brainstorming," not "brain drizzling," to spark bigger, better creativity.
- Celebrate small wins and give praise in progress—never stop!
- Let people know that milestones can be small at first—pay tribute to all meaningful milestones.
- Spread stories, start culture committees, or culture councils that define the culture and unique personality of your organization.
- Reward results and show teams how to relish their successes.
- Let achievers shine and help grow other leaders.
- Allow recognition to go viral.
- Set examples for everyone and be specific about your desired outcomes.
- Encourage boundaryless thinking and solution-finding techniques among teams.
- Give others credit for all of the organization's successes.
- Encourage on-the-spot coaching.
- Identify internal architects who create fast solutions and shape new motivating strategies.

- Champion and appreciate great ideas and hard work.
- Give recognition when it counts by listening closely and paying attention to the little wins along the way—they will eventually lead to bigger successes and blaze the trail for others to follow.
- Notice how hard people are trying and acknowledge it.
- Never stop showing your appreciation for the people around you.
- Laser focus on the aims you want to target and when you hit the bullseye, yell, "I Did It! Bingo!"

Add your own thoughts to this list and share them with your team.

Throughout this book you've learned about the internal and external factors of motivation. You've seen the importance of working with human nature and encouraging entrepreneurial thinking in your employees. You've learned to link motivation to performance and performance to business systems. And you've studied the critical nature and importance of values, humor, synergy, and team power.

Now it's time to bring all of this together in the real world—in your work! After all, it doesn't matter much if you don't put it to use. As I mentioned in the introduction, this isn't a book that was meant just to be *read*— it's a book that was meant to be *used*! The practical and daily application of what's in these pages will make this book a useful and effective management tool for you. Or you can just let the book gather dust on your shelf. It's up to you. And I'd like to hear from you and know about your success stories on the job and how this book has helped to facilitate your success as a manager and leader. Just write to me at: Anne@AnneBruce.com, and I promise to write you back!

It's Either Motivation or Mediocrity

How important is motivation? It makes all the difference. You may be the most knowledgeable, experienced, talented, and capable manager in the world. But if your employees are lacking in motivation, mediocrity will creep into your organization.

Motivation is not a simple matter. In fact, as this book has discussed, motivation involves a lot of elements. If you want to put them all together, consider the following recommendations:

DESIGN, DEVELOP, AND EXPAND APPRECIATION AND RECOGNITION TOOLS

TOOLS

As manager, you have the power to build and create new and exciting experiences for your employees that can shape hundreds of individual and team experiences—on site or around the world. By doing this you can impact every location, every employee, and every situation. Visit OCTanner.com for super great employee recognition and appreciation tools, training, books, and iPhone apps you can't live without. Here are some of their cool recognition suggestions you'll want to consider using:

■ Show employees how to duplicate and relive their successes. Have them create achievement and recognition spaces on their computer, iPad, Blackberry, smart phone, electronic tablet, or on bulletin boards in the office. It's important to give people places to collect and store their achievements and rewards. By doing this, you will give them a place where they can remind themselves of their accomplishments and successes and then start a plan to repeat those successes on a larger scale. Vision boards for future planning and bulletin boards for revisiting an employee's success can be created technologically or tactically.

■ Give recognition plaques, trophies, and acknowledgments that scream "Well Done!" Investigate talking cards, clocks, plaques, and trophies that speak to and reinforce a job well done. Use recognition cards that speak out loud to a person's achievements and say, "Awesome Job!" "Bravo!" "You Did It Once, You Can Do It Again!" Come up with your own recognition gestures appropriate for your company and then tell it like it is.

■ Come up with your own recognition point system. Allow employees to collect points toward gifts and cool prizes, cultural bling that's customized just for them, like engraved watches, initial necklaces, initial rings, personalized pens, tote bags, and more. Make people feel special with customization.

■ It's okay to pamper people once in a while. Give employees a little pampering when it's called for, maybe a spa day, or a weekend at a luxury hotel with their significant other, a night at the symphony or ballet. Focus on things that a person may not take time to do for him- or herself.

■ Go the extra mile for your people—be a wizard of awe, a guru of greatness and excitement, and a master of magical thinking when someone deserves special recognition.

Check out the book, *The Orange Revolution*, by Adrian Gostick and Chester Elton, authors of *The Carrot Principle*, another must-read for managers who want to motivate!

- Invest in employee development and link it to energizing and motivating your people. It's the best investment for any organization.
- Let employees mentor and coach one another for real-world, hands-on learning. It's a good way for employees to develop their skills—and their motivation.
- Prepare your employees to deal with change. Encourage them to think creatively, to solve problems, and to find opportunities.

This chapter is about your imperative to cultivate your human capital. The challenge lies not in the work itself, but in you, the person who creates and manages the work environment.

Be Committed to Developing and Growing Talent

You must be committed to continually developing your people. Employee development can pay big dividends for both the organization and its employees. The organization benefits because its employees have greater skills and are more versatile. The employees benefit because they're becoming better and getting a chance to go above and beyond their normal work activities.

When you give employees the opportunity to learn, develop, and grow, they expand their horizons and make connections. They find new motivation in what they do and in their work environment. If you want to electrify your employees and motivate them to become lifelong learners, consider the words of management guru Peter Drucker, who summed up one of the secrets to success for the founder of IBM, "Thomas Watson trained and trained and trained." Life changes—and the people who don't change along with life are left behind.

IT'S AS SIMPLE AS ABC

SMART

MANAGING

Point A: Organizations that invest in employee development and training have significantly higher market values than those that do not.

Point B: Organizations that encourage employee training and offer opportunities for employees to get involved in learning make greater gains in productivity than those that do not.

Point C: A vital factor in the long-term success of any organization is a healthy and productive relationship between managers and employees.

What kind of development is best? That's a question you've got to answer according to your organization, your needs, and your employees. While some organizations prefer highly structured training environments, others allow employees the freedom to identify and create their own training opportunities, encouraging innovative thinking and problem solving.

In the words of Maya Angelou, "Now that we know better, we must do better." I believe that managers today do know better, because they are savvy, curious, and diligent when it come to motivating and rewarding their people. And when a manager does not know better, for whatever reason, there are no excuses! All of us can find a better way via the Internet, through colleagues we work with, world-class case studies, and volumes of books and programs, like this one, available on the market.

Of real importance are climate, culture, and attitudes in the environment. You can offer the best development opportunities, yet fail to get your employees involved if your environment doesn't show support for employee development. If you don't encourage greater employee participation in the organization, and if you act in ways that show you view development as no more than the acquisition of tools for the job, don't expect your employees to show much interest.

Studies clearly show that in organizations with workplace practices that promote employee involvement, the benefits are significant, for managers as well as employees. These benefits include greater loyalty, improved processes, less waste, more cooperation, and more shared concern for customer satisfaction.

When you encourage employees to be alert for ways to improve practices within your organization, great things happen. It's no wonder that today more than 85 percent of American businesses have some form of employee recognition and rewards program.

Employee Development: An Ongoing Challenge in Good Times and Economically Difficult Times

Employee development can, indeed, be a real challenge for managers—in good times and not-so-good times. What kind of training or education do you currently provide? Do you merely *offer* opportunities? Or do you *promote* them, maybe with some incentives? Do you try to meet organizational needs? Or do you try to engage employee interests? If you want to do both, how do you achieve a proper balance? And what's an appropriate investment of money, time, and other resources?

It's impossible to answer all of these questions for every possible situation, of course. But here are a few ideas to consider:

- **Focus training on needs.** Ask employees what they need to learn before you start any training initiative. Then teach what they need. Design ongoing learning to meet both individual and organizational needs.

- **Be broad-based and flexible.** You can deliver a message in more than one way. Break out of the traditional mold of thinking and start looking into different formats and locations for your training and development.

- **Learning is intentional.** You can create an urgency for learning, but employees must take the initiative. You can't force learning. Make employees accountable for their own personal and professional growth. After every training session, ask attendees to come up with one action item they will act on. Then have them report back specifically on how they brought that action item to the workplace.

- **Don't rely on the facilitator to make learning effective and stick.** Employees should be both learners and teachers. It should not be the responsibility of facilitators or instructors to make employees learn. That's the responsibility of the employees to take the initiative to adapt, delete, modify, or expand on the learning opportunities that have been provided.

- **Get it to them in a timely manner.** Deliver training as close as possible to the time your employees actually need it and will be able to use it. That's when they learn it best, so that's when it will have the greatest impact and deliver the highest return on investment, because they can apply the tools they learn almost immediately.

- **Customize training.** Adapt your training to both individual and organizational needs. Harness the talents of your people. Don't just "spray" them with training and then pray that some of it will stick. The spray-and-pray approach doesn't work in the real world.

■ **Try FIDO.** Unlearn the approaches that don't work. To break bad habits, and help employees to get "unstuck" from past performance problems, use the FIDO approach: Forget It and Drive On! And get people moving again—onward and upward!

LEARNING LABS

TOOLS

Create learning laboratories in your organization. Have employees identify specific skills and knowledge they'd like to gain. Then coordinate and implement ongoing seminars and workshops while researching the best learning resources available. Use learning labs as an effective means of achieving your organization's performance goals.

How will you know if your training program has been worth the investment of money, time, and energy? What benefits will you be able to notice? How will you be able to measure the results in terms of your bottom line? Can you appreciate the other advantages of training?

Here's a quick checklist to help you gain perspective on "practical," "useful," and "meaningful" training in your organization:

■ **Determine your needs.** Survey your employees. Study any performance problems to identify which causes you can remedy through training.

■ **Use the most appropriate trainers.** You get what you pay for when it comes to hiring trainers and facilitators. This is no place to try to save money. Choose trainers with experience in work environments and with needs similar to yours. Look for value-added customization, design, and development skill sets, too. You'll extend the life of your training efforts and get more for your money with trainers who can change things up and create training programs that are timely and cutting edge—helping you to keep your training programs current and exciting—not dull and boring. Remember, if your training programs are boring then so are you!

■ **Help trainers help you.** Whoever you hire will be only as good as his or her knowledge of your needs. Tell facilitators about your situation, your people, your culture—anything that can help him or her serve you better.

- **Have your employees develop action plans.** Make certain that every employee in a training program has an action plan to implement what he or she learns. This should be fairly simple if the training is based on employee needs. There are two reasons driving this recommendation. One, if employees don't use what they learn, they quickly lose it. Two, if employees think in advance about how they'll use what they learn, they'll likely be more interested in the training they get.

- **Include experiential learning.** Many people learn better by doing, especially for work activities. Have your employees apply what they learn as soon as possible. Not only will they learn better, but their feedback will help your training department work more effectively with them.

- **Start with clear objectives.** Before the training begins, communicate your objectives for the program to your leadership, to your employees, and to the trainer. Be specific about what your employees will be able to do as a result of the training. Give employees the chance to influence and direct the thrust of the program. And then make sure they have chances to use their new skills immediately.

- **Meet with employees before they go off to training.** Agree on what results you'd all like to see from the training event. Ask your employees what they hope to gain from the experience. What are their expectations going in? Arrange a time to go over action plans with each of them as soon after the training as possible.

- **Review action plans.** After the training session(s), have each of your employees go over his or her action plan with you. Help people refine their plans. Prepare your employees to make the most of their training. Start a performance coaching program as follow-up.

Organize a Coaching Program

Once you've invested in your employees' learning and development, it's time for coaching to begin.

As a manager, you go to a lot of trouble to keep your copy and scanner machines working, to maintain the computer systems, and to renew maintenance contracts on your printers—among other things. But when it comes to sustaining the motivation of your employees, it's easy to for-

> ## MAKE OBJECTIVES SPECIFIC
> **SMART**
>
> **MANAGING**
>
> What kind of objectives should you set for training? That depends on the type of training. But generally, the more specific the objectives, the better. For example, if your employees are learning a computer program, objectives such as "to be able to import text files into templates" or "to know how to select font types and sizes" are more useful than "to learn about XYZ desktop publishing software."
>
> It's easy for employees to be overwhelmed by information during training. Then, on the job, they can't apply it. If you set objectives in advance, they'll learn in terms of your expectations—so they'll focus better.

get that they too must be "maintained." A coaching program is one effective way to maintain employees' motivation.

Getting everyone to work together is a great way to solve problems and induce innovative thinking on the job. Let's face it: employees working alone (especially if they're new to the job) will hesitate to tell a manager, "I don't understand" or "I made a mistake." However, these same employees might be willing to share their thoughts and feelings with someone else on the team or with a manager who behaves like a coach.

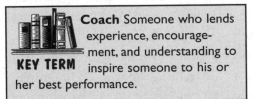

KEY TERM **Coach** Someone who lends experience, encouragement, and understanding to inspire someone to his or her best performance.

Coaching Is Motivating to Coaches, Too!

At a communications company in the Midwest, managers quickly discovered the benefits of putting a coaching program in place.

In this company, each employee volunteered to coach another employee and made a one-year commitment to doing so. The company soon realized that not only did the employees being coached benefit from the program, but the coaches did as well. It was a win-win for all!

Just a few years into the program, almost everyone at the company had volunteered to coach someone. The results? More motivated employees and higher profits. In addition, turnover was substantially lower. The coaching program proved to be one way to keep both employees and managers committed to their work and to the company. They were making a difference.

> ### NAYSAYERS NOT ALLOWED
>
> **CAUTION**
>
> Beware of coaches who complain, whine, or grumble along with employees. These are not coaches—they're negative cheerleaders. They're not likely to help the employee perform better or feel more motivated. Check out the attitude of a potential coach before assigning him or her to an employee.
>
> Research shows that a negative perception of your organization during the first 60 to 90 days of employment can lead new hires to look for another job within the first year!

Disney Keeps New-Hire Orientation Motivating!

According to the Society for Human Resource Management, U.S. employers invest considerable time and money in the orientation of new hires. The organization reported that more than 80 percent of companies offer orientation for new hires. This study also reports that acclimating new hires to corporate culture is becoming an increasingly popular retention strategy.

There's something impressive about the Disney organization: all training begins with building pride and morale. Keeping employees motivated through training and coaching is an important part of the incredibly successful Disney culture.

The first few days of training are spent recognizing and respecting Disney traditions. New hires attend what is called a "Disney Traditions Class," where they learn about

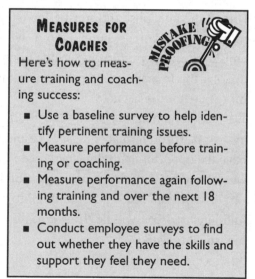

MEASURES FOR COACHES

MISTAKE PROOFING

Here's how to measure training and coaching success:

- Use a baseline survey to help identify pertinent training issues.
- Measure performance before training or coaching.
- Measure performance again following training and over the next 18 months.
- Conduct employee surveys to find out whether they have the skills and support they feel they need.

the history, philosophy, values, and high-quality guest services Disney is known for worldwide.

What happens next integrates Magic Kingdom–style coaching with human nature. Depending on the position, cast members begin training "on-the-job," not in a classroom, for the following two days to two weeks.

Check Out Disney Institute

If you don't work for Disney, you can still benefit from their motivational training.

Disney Institute was created to easily adapt Disney Best Practices to other organizations. Here learners are shown how to step into a "living laboratory" at various Disney Theme Parks and Resorts for guided behind-the-scenes field experiences. Disney's brand of business excellence is also being taught at locations across the U.S. and, to date, in more than 45 countries.

Whether you tune into a Disney Institute WebCast, attend a workshop in your city, or immerse yourself in a multiday program at a Disney Destination, the lessons developed are rooted in the time-tested visions and ideals of Walt Disney himself.

Find Out What Employees Love to Do

One of the cheapest and most effective ways to tap into an employee's motivation involves figuring out which tasks or assignments an employee enjoys performing. When possible, reward employees by minimizing the less enjoyable tasks and giving them an opportunity to do more of what they love to do.

Remember that one of the 12 questions from Gallup rated affirmatively by high-performing, highly engaged employees to ask is this: "At work, do you have the opportunity to do what you do best every day?" Or, as Confucius wisely stated: "Find a job you love and you'll never work a day in your life."

Find out the tasks that your employees find gratifying, rewarding and fulfilling, and you will be thrilled at how motivated they are to perform high-quality work!

Second, ask employees for their opinions . . . and then implement as many of them as you can.

Think of it this way: is it easier to drive from the front or the back seat of the car? It's pretty obvious, right? The front seat has the best view of the road. The *backseat driver* may have an opinion, but he certainly doesn't have the best view of the road.

Likewise, you might need to use consultants from time to time to come in from the outside to help you fix things that you can't quite see.

But unless they're specialists in their fields, they're more like backseat drivers compared to your own employees! After all, your employees are likely closest to the work, the customer, the product, and so on.

When you don't ask employees for their opinions and when you don't include their feedback on how work gets done, you are ignoring *free* consultation from subject-matter experts.

Oh, and why I'm including this concept here is because asking employees for their opinions and implementing them is a proven strategy to increase engagement levels.

Think about it. When you make a decision for yourself as opposed to being pressured into one, aren't you more likely to stand behind it even when things get hard? That's part of human nature. So when a work process or flow changes, doesn't it stand to reason that employees have an easier time getting on board when they had a hand in creating the change?

But before you cut a slit in a cardboard box and slap a sign on it saying "Suggestion Box," here's a little caution: asking for suggestions does more harm than good if the suggestions don't lead to changes. "Leaders tend to make two errors regarding employee opinions. The most obvious error involves not asking for them. You're leaving money on the table if you fail to tap into the insights and experience from the people who are closest to the work," says employee engagement expert Scott Carbonara. "The second and worse error is to ask for opinions … and then ignore them," he concludes.

To avoid falling into that pit, I suggest that you don't accept anonymous suggestions. If someone has an idea, have your employee own it by putting his or her name on it. If you can use the suggestion, make sure the person knows how grateful you are that the suggestion was made and tell the person how you are going to use it. Then give that person credit to increase engagement levels even more. But when you can't use a suggestion, having the person's name will allow you to follow up with him or her to say informatively why the idea can't be used at the present time. Acknowledge the effort in making the suggestion.

You Can Be a Motivating Manager!

Any organization can be knocked to its knees by changing circumstances if it isn't taking specific steps to positively prepare for its future through the attitudes, motivation, and actions of its employees. That's what this book has been all about. If you use it properly, it can be a powerful management tool that will keep you and your employees from falling victim to mediocrity and complacency.

But ultimately, none of these principles and examples will be worth more than the paper pulp used to make the pages unless you can translate them into actions that affect employee behaviors. That's what being a motivating manager is all about.

Your skills and talents have already gotten you to this point: you're a manager. Now, apply the ideas and strategies in this book so that you can become an even more successful and effective leader—a motivating manager!

Manager's Checklist for Chapter 12

☑ Create a sense of belonging and greater purpose for your employees.

☑ Dig deep for ways to help employees become self-motivated.

☑ Show employees how to duplicate and live their success!

☑ Pamper people when they deserve it.

☑ Commit to continually developing your employees. The organization benefits because your employees become more skilled. Your employees benefit because they're improving and because they get an opportunity to learn and grow, to expand their horizons and make connections, and to find new motivation.

☑ The kind of development matters less than your environment. Show support for employee development and encourage greater employee participation in the organization with enthusiastic, fun, engaging, and cutting-edge training that entertains and rivets people.

☑ Provide training that's useful and meaningful. First, determine your needs. Then, hire the most appropriate trainers and facilitators and tell them about your needs, situation, people, and culture. Have your employees develop action plans. Set clear objectives. Meet with your employees before they start training to agree on expectations. Finally, after the training, review action plans.

☑ Follow up with a performance-coaching program.

☑ Employee development begins with training, but it should continue with coaching.

☑ Involve employees by allowing them to do more of what they love and make suggestions as your internal experts.

☑ Here's a Ralph Waldo Emerson quote to share with employees: "Make the most of yourself, for that is all there is of you." Now that's motivating.

Index

About the Author

Anne Bruce dispenses humor, wisdom, wit, and practical insights taken from her worldwide travels and life-altering adventures, both in her books and from the speaker's platform and international seminar stage. She has built a global reputation as a disarming and impactful human behaviorist, entertaining speaker on leadership motivation, advocate of America's global talent, and bestselling author of more than 16 books … and counting.

For Anne, every year is a magical year—teaching that our thoughts and words all take part in shaping the future. Anne can't speak enough, or write enough, about the power of passionate people, igniting human potential, growing and branding extraordinary talent, everyday miracles, and the unflappable attitudes that inspire and align organizations and their people to levels of success they never dreamed possible.

Anne has had the privilege to speak, write, or train for prestigious organizations, such as: the White House, the Pentagon, Saks Fifth Avenue, Sony International, Accenture, BestBuy, Coca-Cola, GEICO, Southwest Airlines, Harvard Law School and Stanford Law School, MedAmerica Billing Services, Inc., Sprint, The Conference Board of Europe, Go Positive!™ University!, Ben & Jerry's, JetBlue, Baylor University Medical Center, The Southern Company, American Society of Training and Development (ASTD), the Ritz-Carlton Hotels, Social Security Administration, American Management Association (AMA), Society of Human Resource Management (SHRM), and the American Red Cross.

An acclaimed, bestselling author, whose books have been translated into more than 24 languages, Anne has books published on both personal and professional development, including the award-winning, life-coaching book *Discover True North: A 4-Week Approach to Ignite Your Passion and Activate Your Potential* (McGraw-Hill), *Be Your Own Mentor* (McGraw-Hill), *Motivating Employees* (McGraw-Hill), *Solving Employee Performance Problems: How to Spot Problems Early, Take Appropriate Action, and Bring Out the Best in Everyone* (McGraw-Hill), *Building a High Morale Workplace* (McGraw-Hill), *How to Motivate Every Employee* (McGraw-Hill), *Leaders— Start to Finish: A Roadmap for Training and Developing Leaders at All Levels* (ASTD Press), *Perfect Phrases for Documenting Employee Performance Problems* (McGraw-Hill), *Perfect Phrases for Employee Development Plans* (McGraw-Hill), and *Speak for A Living: The Insider's Guide to Building a Speaking Career* (ASTD Press).

Anne has appeared on the *CBS Evening News* and as a guest on the *Charlie Rose Show*. She's worked extensively in broadcast journalism and has contributed interviews to NBC, MSNBC, ABC, FOX, and CNN news programs. She's been written about in distinguished print media, including *USA Today*, *The San Francisco Examiner*, the *Times* (London), *The Wall Street Journal*, the *San Jose Mercury News*, and numerous magazines, including *Newsweek*, and a variety of international publications.

Anne and her husband, David, enjoy living the beach life in the greater Los Angeles area. Anne is currently writing her first novel and screenplay and a new book titled *Anne-ecdotes to Discovering Your True North*.

Bring this book's training program into your organization. For information on keynote speeches, workshops, and training programs associated with this book and others, visit Anne's website at www.AnneBruce.com. For details on how you can bring this book's training program on *Motivating and Developing Superstar Talent*, from her popular training series *America's Got Talent in the Workplace … And It Comes from All Over the World!* to your organization; additional leadership seminars, or for fees, availability, and scheduling press interviews, please call 214-507-8242, or e-mail Anne@AnneBruce.com for more information.